VOLCANOES

Geology is largely history, but volcanoes are as current as life and
death. Spirit Lake, formed during eruptions of Mount St. Helens
about 1000 B.C., was alive with spring on May 12, 1980, and
undisturbed by small new eruptions from the volcano's summit.
(Photograph by U.S. Geological Survey.)

On May 18, 1980, a giant explosive eruption and avalanche destroyed the entire region surrounding Spirit Lake below Mount St. Helens in moments. Not a tree is left standing; everywhere is barrenness. But Earth abides; life will return to Spirit Lake over the centuries as it did before. (Photograph by the U.S. Geological Survey.)

VOLCANOES

REVISED AND UPDATED EDITION

Robert Decker

Barbara Decker

W. H. FREEMAN AND COMPANY
New York

Library of Congress Cataloging-in-Publication Data

Decker, Robert Wayne, 1927–
   Volcanoes / Robert Decker and Barbara Decker. — Rev. and expanded ed.
     p.   cm.
   Bibliography: p.
   Includes index.
   ISBN 0-7167-1851-0
   1. Volcanoes.   I. Decker, Barbara, 1929– .   II. Title.
QE521.D32 1989   89-31441
551.2′1 — dc20   CIP

Printed in the United States of America

5 6 7 8 9 0 VB 9 9 8 7 6 5 4

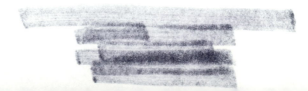

Contents

. . . .

Preface

. . . .

Volcanoes assail the senses. They are beautiful in repose and awesome in eruption; they hiss and roar, they smell of brimstone. Their heat warms, their fires consume; they are the homes of gods and goddesses.

Volcanoes are described in words and pictures, but they must be experienced to be known. Their roots reach deep inside the Earth; their products are scattered in the sky. Understanding volcanoes is an unconquered challenge. This book poses more questions than answers; such is the harvest of curiosity.

Any book about volcanoes is bound to be highly descriptive, but we have tried to look behind these spectacular phenomena and to emphasize the processes involved. Our book is written for anyone — from student to expert — who is interested in learning more about how volcanoes work.

The Bibliography reflects only part of our debt to the hundreds of students of volcanoes whose general knowledge of volcanic processes and products we have used. Three friends deserve our special thanks: James G. Moore of the U.S. Geological Survey, the late Allan Cox of Stanford University, and the late John Staples of W. H. Freeman and Company. Without their help and encouragement the first edition of this book would not have been written.

Active Volcanoes of the World

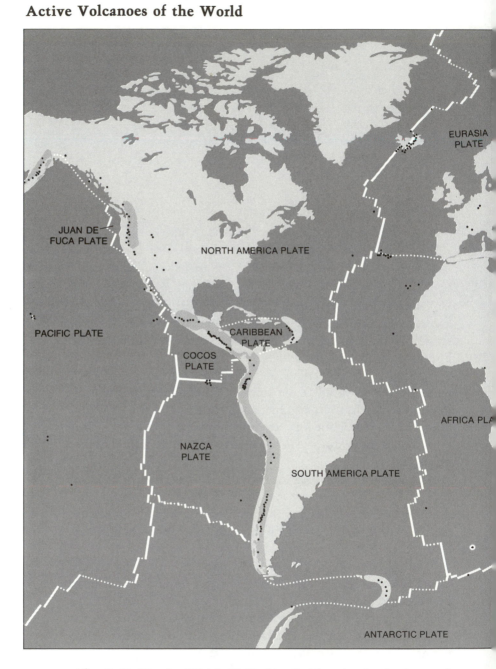

After L. D. Morris, NOAA; T. Simkin, Smithsonian Institution; and
H. Meyers, NOAA; Volcanoes of the World (map), NOAA, 1979.

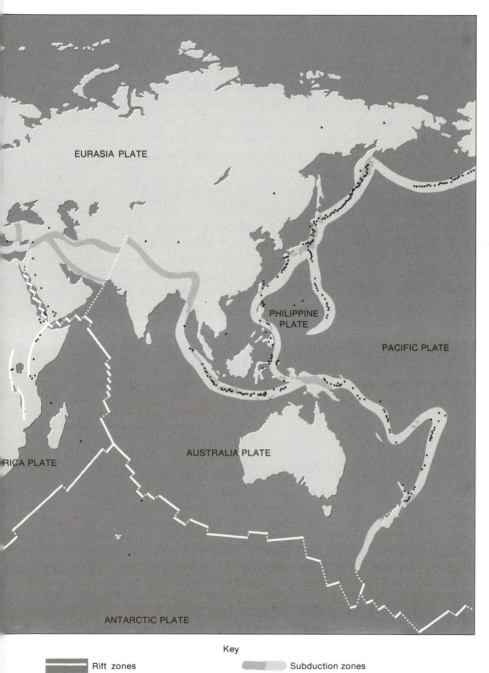

EURASIA PLATE

PHILIPPINE
PLATE

PACIFIC PLATE

AFRICA PLATE

AUSTRALIA PLATE

ANTARCTIC PLATE

Key

 Rift zones   Subduction zones

Strike-slip (transform) faults   • Geologically young volcanoes

In the eight years since *Volcanoes* was first published there has been a great increase in public interest and awareness about volcanism. One hundred twenty volcanoes have erupted, most more than once; 28,000 people were killed by those eruptions or by their immediate aftermath. The fact that the most lethal eruptions during this period were from volcanoes not on our original list of "The World's 101 Most Notorious Volcanoes" is another sign that volcanology is still an evolving science.

But there has been good news during these years, too. Scientists have had some notable successes in forecasting explosive eruptions, thus saving thousands of lives. Thanks to Kilauea Volcano, the Island of Hawaii is at least 400,000 square meters larger than it was 8 years ago, with new black sand beaches kilometers long. Most importantly, new ideas, new discoveries, and worldwide cooperation have helped geologists add more pieces to the puzzle of how volcanoes work.

April 1989   **Robert Decker**
                                                 Barbara Decker

VOLCANOES

Introduction

....

Most of the Earth's mountains, valleys, and plains have been slowly sculptured by uplift and erosion over the last million years, and these in turn have formed from other landscapes long vanished. Volcanoes, though, operate on a different time scale.

On the morning of May 18, 1980, Mount St. Helens in Washington State was a tall, conical volcano 2950 meters high; by nightfall it was an ugly stump of a mountain 2550 meters high, with a cloud of gas and ash rising from a new horseshoe-shaped crater (Color Plates 15 and 16). A massive avalanche had torn away the whole north side of the mountain, unleashing a giant steam explosion that shattered the mountaintop, devastated a forest of 10 million trees, and killed 57 people. A huge eruption cloud jetted upward from the volcano, blanketing central Washington with 2 to 3 inches of ash, and moving as far as the East Coast in 3 days.

Volcanologists from all over the world converged on Washington State. A concerted effort was immediately under way to find answers to the specific questions of just what happened and why, as well as the larger questions of how the lessons learned at Mount St. Helens could be used at other dangerous volcanoes. Both applied and basic research benefited. Volcano monitoring tools and techniques were refined, and assessment of volcanic hazards in other potentially active areas was greatly increased.

The explosion of Mount St. Helens caught the rapt attention of the public, too, as Americans who had thought of a volcanic eruption as something that happened in a Flintstones cartoon suddenly found volcanic ash sifting down into their backyards. They looked for answers to such questions as: Why are volcanoes like Mount St. Helens explosive while others, like those in Hawaii, pour out quieter streams and fountains of lava? Why do volcanoes occur in chains like the Cascade Range or the Japanese islands? How does one know when a volcano is dead and not just dormant?

Mount St. Helens was still in the public consciousness when, five years later, another volcanic catastrophe shocked the world. In November 1985, Nevado del Ruiz Volcano in Colombia erupted, triggering mudflows that raced down its steep valley, engulfing a whole town and killing 25,000 people.

In the aftermath of this tragedy, in addition to studying the details of the actual eruption, scientists focused attention on the problems of reducing volcanic risk by improved monitoring of hazardous volcanoes and by the use of more effective techniques for forecasting eruptions. Also of major concern has been the sensitive social/political problem of how and when to issue a forecast of a disaster that may or may not happen.

Besides giving a basic description of the latest theories of how volcanoes work, this book addresses the issues and concerns mentioned here. We start with the question of why volcanoes are common in some regions of the Earth and not in others.

1
Seams of the Earth

1   San Andreas fault cutting across the Elkhorn and Carrizo Plains in south-central California. The North America plate is on the right and the Pacific plate is on the left. Movement on the fault is right lateral, so called because for a person standing on either plate, the sense of motion on the opposite plate is to the right. (Photograph by Robert E. Wallace, U.S. Geological Survey.)

Nature knows no pause in progress and development,
and attaches her curse to all inaction.

—GOETHE (1749–1832)

. . . .

The matching shores of eastern South America and western Africa form an intriguing jigsaw puzzle. Did Brazil's bulge once fit against the Congo? Did some great supercontinent break up and drift apart, each piece forming one of our present continents?

Alfred Wegener, an Austrian scientist, championed the concept of continental drift for 20 years until his death on the Greenland Icecap in 1930. He noted not only that the edges of the continents make a rough fit, but also that the Appalachian mountain range in eastern North America breaks off abruptly in Newfoundland and reappears across the Atlantic Ocean in Ireland, Scotland, and Scandinavia. He argued that the similarity of European and American fossils until 180 million years ago and the dissimilarity of more recent fossils is one more piece of evidence that the continents as we know them are still-drifting segments of an ancient supercontinent.

Wegener also recognized that the Earth's surface has two predominant elevations: one between sea level and 1000 meters above sea level, the other between 4000 and 5000 meters below sea level (Figure 2). He hypothesized that this difference in elevation between continents and oceans was caused by differences in the density and thickness of rocks in the continental blocks compared to oceanic crust. He believed that the lighter and thicker continental blocks floated above the oceanic crust like icebergs drifting through the sea.

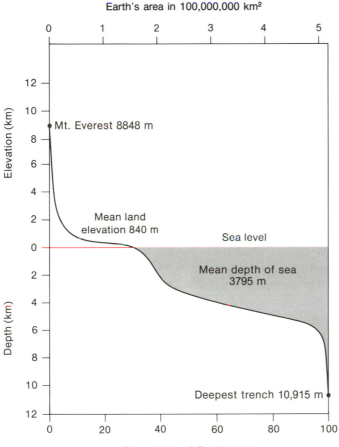

2 Graph comparing the Earth's surface elevations and surface areas. The two benches on the curve reflect the basically different thicknesses and densities of continental and oceanic crust. (Adapted from Alyn C. Duxbury, *The Earth and Its Oceans.* © 1971 Addison-Wesley, Reading, Massachusetts. Fig. 3.2, Reprinted with permission.)

To understand his use of "float" and "drift," one must understand the geologist's concepts of crust and time. We-gener envisioned the oceanic crust as being more viscous than tar or pitch, so that the "floating" took thousands of years to reach balance, and the "drifting" proceeded even more slowly.

Continental drift was one of the great scientific controversies of its day, and Wegener's arguments in favor of it were alluring. Wegener called the great supercontinent he envisioned Pangaea: it was so large that it contained both the polar scars of ancient ice ages and the equatorial legacy of vast coal swamps which existed before its breakup. According to his theory, the present locations of glacial deposits near the equator and of coal deposits near the current poles are the result of continental drift.

But Wegener was also a zealot, and many of his contemporaries, wary of too much zeal, considered him a crackpot. Geophysicists specializing in the study of the Earth's interior in the first quarter of this century were especially skeptical because Wegener was unable to identify the strong forces needed to propel the continents away from each other. These experts had already concluded that the interior of the Earth was as solid and strong as steel. To them, the notion that floating continents could drift through such a strong "sea" seemed untenable.

Their knowledge of the deep interior of the Earth came mainly from analyzing what happens to earthquake waves as they propagate through the Earth. This approach to Earth science is called seismology. Its methods are similar to the doctor's technique of thumping on your chest to discover whether there is liquid or air in your lungs; differences in the quality of the thump sound passing through your chest provide the key. Seismology is a rigorous discipline based on precise physical principles and its conclusions are well respected by all geologists. The denial of continental drift on such geophysical objections was convincing despite the good circumstantial evidence in its favor, and the hypothesis went underground for 30 years.

However, among geologists there is a half-joke called Smith's Law, which states that anything that did happen, can happen. So even without understanding how the large horizontal movement of continents could happen, some geologists still looked for evidence that it did happen.

The breakthrough that proved Wegener was right came in 1960 from marine geophysicists analyzing the Earth's magnetic field over the ocean floor. They found that the magnetic field was unusually strong directly over the oceanic ridges. The reason, they proposed, is that the rocks making up the ridge contain iron-rich minerals and are magnetized parallel to the Earth's magnetic field, which tends to reinforce that field.

As the geophysicists extended their surveys away from the ridges, they found that the magnetic field at the surface of the sea was a zebra-striped pattern of alternating belts of unusually high and unusually low intensity. Their explanation of the low-intensity belts was that the ocean floor beneath them had formed at times when the Earth's magnetic field pointed to the south, rather than to the north as it does today.

By the time of the marine magnetic surveys in 1960, geophysicists studying the magnetic properties and ages of lavas on land had already demonstrated that the Earth's magnetic field periodically switches from north to south and back again. The time between reversals may be as short as 30,000 years or as long as several million years. Using this magnetic reversal time scale, the marine geophysicists knew when the field had flipped, and they could estimate the age of the ocean floor beneath each magnetic stripe. The stage was set for a dramatic new idea.

Geologists now proposed that instead of continents drifting *through* the ocean floor, the seafloor spread away from the oceanic ridges as it formed, carrying the continents along as part of large, spreading plates (Figure 3). The new idea was called seafloor spreading or *plate tectonics*, and the magnetic stripes gave a record of both the geometry and the rate of spreading, or plate movements. The pattern and ages of the magnetic stripes parallel to the ocean's ridge systems provide a giant slow-motion tape recording of the Earth's horizontal movements over the past 170 million years.

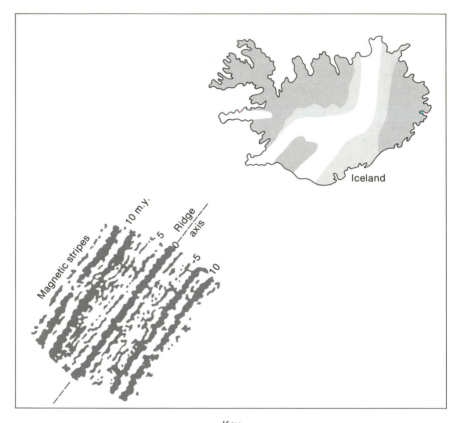

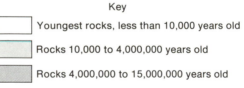

Key

☐ Youngest rocks, less than 10,000 years old

☐ Rocks 10,000 to 4,000,000 years old

☐ Rocks 4,000,000 to 15,000,000 years old

m.y.   Millions of years

3 Magnetic field strength measured at the sea surface southwest of Iceland shows a definite striped pattern parallel to the axis of the Mid-Atlantic Ridge. The symmetry of the pattern on either side of the ridge and the similar pattern in the ages of volcanic rocks in Iceland are strong evidence that the seafloor spreads away from the ridge axis. (After Charles Drake, "The Geological Revolution," Condon Lectures, Oregon State System of Higher Education, Eugene, Oregon, 1970.)

The pattern that has emerged shows the Earth's surface broken into about 12 plates that are moving in various directions relative to one another. The margins or seams between the plates are of three basic types: *compressional*, where the plates override one another; *extensional*, where the plates break apart; and side-slipping or *strike-slip*, where the plates slide by one another without separating or overriding (Figures 4 and 5). Compressional and extensional margins are characterized by different types of volcanic activity and strike-slip margins by almost no volcanism, so the link between plate tectonics and volcanism is close indeed.

Earthquakes, topography, and other geological structures identify the three types of seams. At the compressional margins, also known as *subduction zones*, one plate, generally oceanic, pushes beneath the other. This causes earthquakes originating near the surface seam or in the sinking plate at depths as great as 700 kilometers. Physical forces at the compressional margin cause the ocean floor to bend down into a deep trench while the edge of the upper plate is pushed into folds, or broken by thrust faults. Rock layers scraped off the ocean floor are stacked into slices or folded against the upper plate. The geological result is an island arc like Japan or a mountain chain like the Andes.

At extensional margins, the earthquakes are shallow and follow the center of the rift. The center of the rift is often a valley formed by the separating plates (Figure 6). No folds are formed because the area is being stretched, not squeezed, and the fractures are either open cracks or slumps called normal faults. Most extensional margins are submarine, and new oceanic crust is formed at the separating edges; the crust grows outward from the oceanic ridges near the centers of the world's major oceans. The main ridges are the Mid-Atlantic ridge, the East Pacific Rise, and the Indian Ocean ridges. They are broad, rugged, submarine mountain ranges a few kilometers high, a few thousand kilometers wide, and tens of thousands of kilometers long. Drain away the oceans and you would be able to see the greatest mountain system on the Earth.

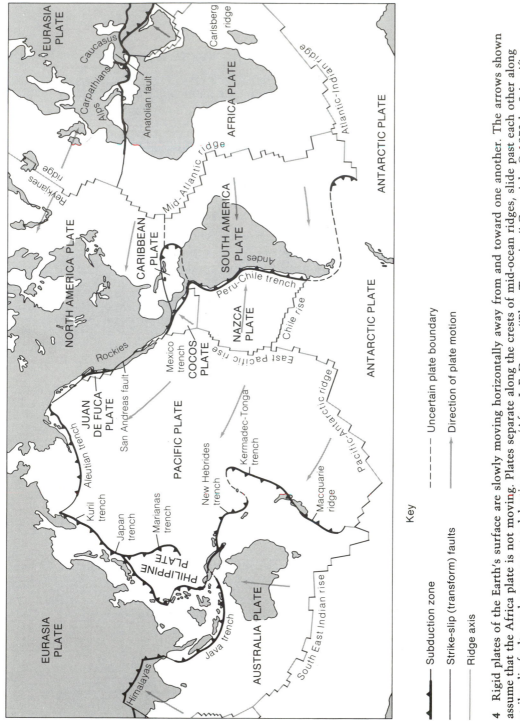

4 Rigid plates of the Earth's surface are slowly moving horizontally away from and toward one another. The arrows shown assume that the Africa plate is not moving. Plates separate along the crests of mid-ocean ridges, slide past each other along strike-slip faults, and converge at subduction zones. (After J. F. Dewey, "Plate Tectonics." Copyright © 1972 by Scientific American, Inc. All rights reserved.)

Key

— Subduction zone

— Strike-slip (transform) faults

— Ridge axis

- - - Uncertain plate boundary

→ Direction of plate motion

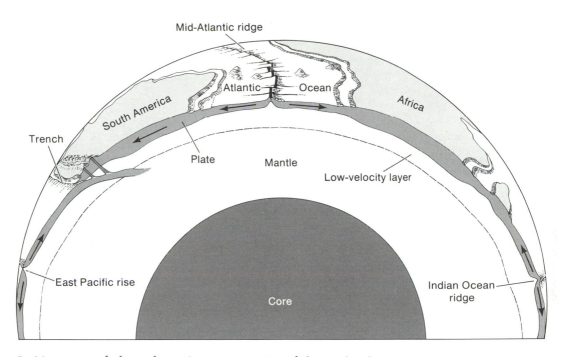

5 Movement of plates shown in a cross section of the Earth. The Africa and South America plates separate along the Mid-Atlantic Ridge at a rate of a few inches per year. The South America and Nazca (East Pacific Ocean) plates converge to form the Andes Mountains. The thickness of the plates and the low-velocity layer on which they move are exaggerated so that they can be shown at this small scale. (After K. C. Burke and J. Tuzo Wilson, "Hot Spots on the Earth's Surface." Copyright © 1976 by Scientific American, Inc. All rights reserved.)

The strike-slip plate margins (called *transform faults* in the jargon of plate tectonics) are also mainly submarine. They connect offsets of the oceanic ridges into a rectangular pattern that looks like an alligator's hide on topographical maps of the seafloor (Figure 7).

Sometimes a slice of continent gets involved in the shearing of a side-slipping margin; the San Andreas fault in California is the classic example of a transform fault on land. Los Angeles is moving northwest relative to San Francisco at a

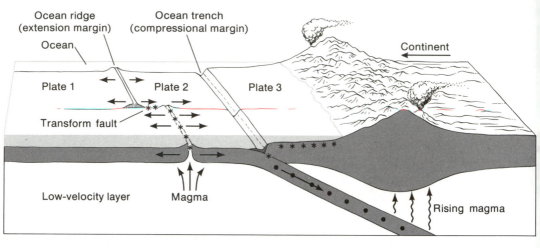

Key

* Shallow earthquakes
  (tension on ridges; lateral slip on transform faults)

• Deep earthquakes
  (mainly showing thrusting and down-dip compression)

6   Schematic cross section of plate margins showing the association of earthquakes with the plate boundaries formed by ocean ridges, strike-slip (transform) faults, and subduction zones. (After L. Sykes et al., in F. Press and R. Siever, *Earth*, First Edition, p. 644. W. H. Freeman and Company, Copyright © 1974.)

7   Topographical map of the Atlantic Ocean with the water drained away. The Mid-Atlantic Ridge is one of the world's greatest mountain ranges. The breaks perpendicular to the valley crest of the ridge are called fracture zones or transform faults — other terms for strike-slip margins. (From *World Ocean Floor Panorama* by Bruce C. Heezen and Marie Tharp, initiated and supported by the Office of Naval Research. Copyright Marie Tharp, 1977. Reproduced by permission of Marie Tharp, all rights reserved.)

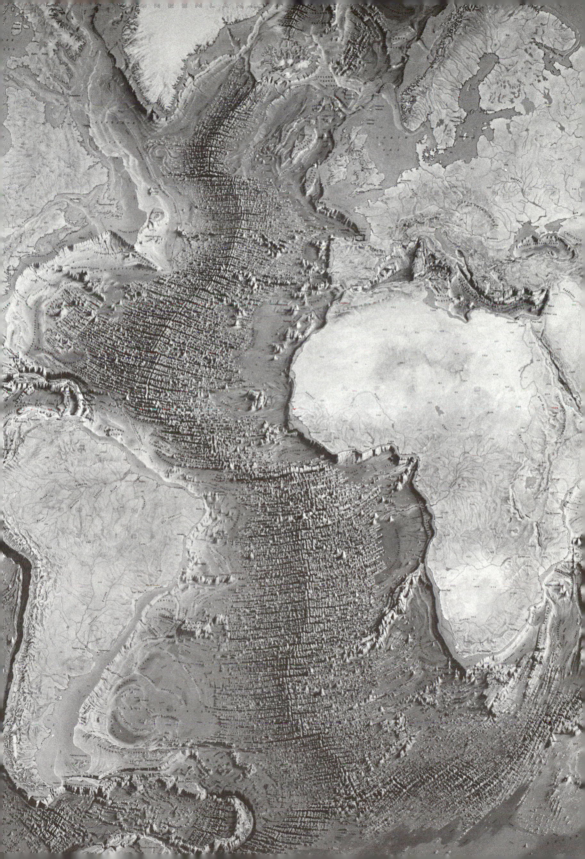

rate of about 5 centimeters per year. However, society will probably make them one city long before nature slides the two together. Shallow earthquakes, linear valleys, and twisted rocks mark the strike-slip plate margins (Figure 1).

Despite the overwhelming evidence that seafloor spreading takes place, the strength and solidity of the Earth's interior remained a problem that seismologists have only recently resolved. This is ironic since it was the seismologists whose arguments had shot down Wegener's hypothesis in the 1920s. Looking closely at earthquake wave records, particularly those from underground nuclear bomb tests with precisely known locations and times of origin, they discovered a zone about 100 to 200 kilometers beneath the Earth's surface where seismic waves travel unusually slowly and are partially absorbed.

This low-velocity layer is not very strong; it probably contains a small percentage of molten rock. The characteristics of this layer provide a reasonable explanation for plate motions and for the deep source of volcanoes. The plates move on the soft, low-velocity layer under the influence of small horizontal forces, and fractures in the Earth's crust at the extensional plate margins allow the partially molten rock to leak to the surface, forming volcanoes (Figure 8).

Wegener turned out to be a prophet, although his original idea has been significantly changed. He believed the continents drifted like isolated rafts through a viscous oceanic crust. The theory of seafloor spreading envisions rigid plates of oceanic crust forming and spreading from the ocean ridges; the continental blocks are carried like rafts frozen into the larger plates, which are composed of both oceanic and continental crust.

In the last 3 decades of unprecedented progress in our understanding of the Earth, the development and rapid acceptance of the concept of seafloor spreading stands as one of the grand moments in science. Not only can the jigsaw puzzle of the continents be reconstructed, but their ongoing movements can be determined. The dynamics of plate motions control both earthquakes and volcanoes, which occur for the most part on the creaking and leaking margins of the plates.

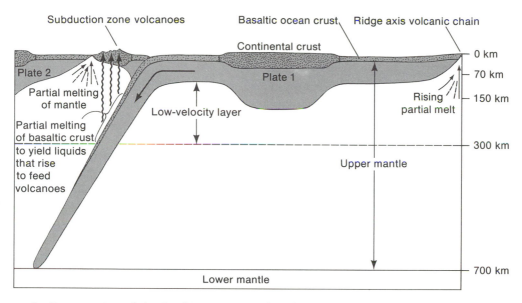

8   Cross section of the Earth's upper mantle. The rigid plate is composed of solidified rock that moves on the partially molten low-velocity layer. The plates are approximately 70 kilometers thick under oceans and 100 to 150 kilometers thick under continents. The continents are parts of the plates and move with them. (After J. F. Dewey, "Plate Tectonics." Copyright © 1972 by Scientific American, Inc. All rights reserved.)

The association between volcanoes and earthquake belts has long been recognized. Aristotle proposed that earthquakes were caused by the rumbling of pent-up gases which were eventually vented at volcanoes; he recognized the connection even though we wouldn't agree with his explanation today. Perhaps the most important lesson of the past 30 years has been the virtue of scientific humility: Who knows which ideas that now appear untenable will turn out to be right, and which of those ideas that we currently accept on the basis of available evidence will seem hopelessly naive 2000 years from now?

2

Surtsey, Iceland

9 Lightning bolts discharge the buildup of electricity in the
uprushing ash column at Surtsey. Ninety-second time exposure.
(Photograph by Sigurgeir Jónasson, December 1, 1963.)

*At three o'clock in the morning we saw smoke rising
from the sea and thought it to be land; but on closer
consideration we concluded that this was a special
wonder wrought by God and that a natural sea could burn.*

—CAPTAIN JORGEN MINDELBERG
ICELAND (1783)

. . . .

Iceland sits astride the Mid-Atlantic Ridge, part of the worldwide rift system. This 300-by-500-kilometer island whose north shore touches the Arctic Circle is entirely volcanic in origin. Eruptions occur about every 5 years; sometimes from distinct volcanoes like Mount Hekla, which has erupted 20 times since A.D. 900 but often from long fissures that erupt only once. Iceland grows in size from volcanic eruptions, and is worn away by the storms of the North Atlantic. Icelandic farmers and fishermen know the Earth is a dynamic place; they are all geologists at heart.

The story of the Surtsey eruption begins at sea. The late Icelandic volcanologist Sigurdur Thorarinsson was its chronicler.

At 7:15 A.M. on November 14, 1963, Olafur Vestmann, the cook on a fishing boat off the south coast of Iceland, noticed dark smoke on the horizon against the half-light of dawn. Since no land existed in that direction the first alarm was that a ship was on fire, but soon the fishermen recognized that the black columns of volcanic ash signaled an eruption from beneath the sea. By 11:00 A.M. the eruption cloud of ash and steam had reached a height of 3500 meters, and volcanologists were on their way to observe the eruption from the air.

At 11:30 A.M. the eruption was coming from three submarine vents along a northeast–southwest line. Explosions from the vents were occurring every few seconds, shooting jets of dense black ash to heights of 100 to 150 meters. By 3:00 P.M. the separate eruption columns had joined along a 500-meter line across the sea surface, and the rapid emission of black volcanic debris indicated that a new island was about to form. Surtsey, named for Surtur, the mythological giant of fire, was born that night (Figure 10).

The eruption was a surprise. Only in hindsight were the few clues to a forthcoming eruption recognized. Two days before the eruption, a marine research vessel had noticed a strange rise in the temperature of the sea surface above the normal 7 to 9°C in an area about 3 kilometers from the eruption site. Also on November 12, people in Vik, a coastal village 80 kilometers to the east, had noticed the rotten-egg smell of hydrogen sulfide. The seismograph at Reykjavik, 120 kilometers away, had recorded weak tremors a week before the eruption was first observed, but the location of the seismic disturbance could not be determined. No preliminary earthquakes were felt at the fishing port of Vestmannaeyjar on Heimaey Island, 22 kilometers northeast of Surtsey, the closest settlement to the eruption (Figure 11).

Presumably the eruption began quietly at 130 meters below sea level and took days or weeks to build the volcano to just beneath the sea surface. There, the explosive activity could no longer be contained and quenched by the pressure and chill of the sea.

During the first week, the new island erupted and grew almost continuously. Closely spaced explosions merging into a steady jetting of volcanic ash formed a towering column that rose to a height of 9 kilometers.

By November 18, Surtsey was a ridge 550 meters long and 45 meters high, split lengthwise by the erupting fissure. Gradually one vent along the fissure became dominant and the island began to grow more circular. On November 24 the island was 900 meters long and 650 meters wide, and the rim of the main crater was almost 100 meters high. The entire

10 Column of steam and ash rising over 3000 meters from the Surtsey eruption on November 16, 1963, two days after the eruption was first sighted. (Photograph by Hjálmar Bárdarson.)

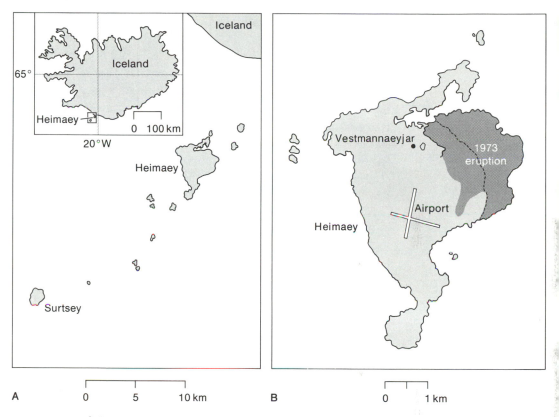

11 *A.* Map of the Vestmann Islands showing Surtsey, which formed in 1963–1967, and Heimaey, which formed in prehistoric times. *B.* The shaded area represents lava added to Heimaey during the 1973 eruption. The former shore is shown by a dashed line.

island was built of loose dark volcanic debris, thrown out in fragments by the explosive eruptions. Lava flows of liquid rock had not yet begun, and the loose volcanic pile was an easy target for the strong winter storms of the North Atlantic. However, the eruption more than kept pace with marine erosion and slumping. By February 5, 1964, the maximum height of the volcanic island was 174 meters and the maximum diameter 1300 meters, including a wave-cut terrace around the shore with a width of about 150 meters.

During the first 3 months of the eruption, the sea had easy access to the erupting vents, both by direct flooding and by seepage through the loose volcanic pile. This contact with water produced the steam explosions that characterize shallow submarine eruptions. Each explosion expelled a black mass of rock fragments, out of which shot numerous larger fragments of pasty lava called volcanic bombs. The bombs left trails of black volcanic ash that rapidly turned white and furry as the hot, invisible steam in the trails cooled and condensed. The black jetlike arcs turning grayish white gave the eruptions the appearance of an exploding fireworks factory (Figure 12). The bombs whistled as they spun in flight, and often landed in the sea more than a kilometer from the vent. The steam explosions themselves were peculiarly quiet, beginning with a muted thump and an almost silent burst of debris.

When the explosions occurred in rapid sequence, as they often did, a large ash and steam cloud rose above the island. On the rare calm days this plume reached as high as 10 kilometers, but generally the strong winds bent the column at 500 to 2000 meters and caused ashfalls many kilometers downwind, some of which contaminated the water supply caught on the roofs in Vestmannaeyjar. The violent updrafts of air into the ash cloud caused whirlwinds, waterspouts, lightning flashes, and sometimes hailstones of falling volcanic fragments coated with ice (Figure 9).

At times the explosive eruptions changed into a continuous uprush of volcanic fragments and steam. Bombs, glowing red to orange, lit the uprushing column at night. Only brief lulls in the eruption occurred during November and December, but by January there were periods of repose lasting up to a day. As the island grew, seawater was more effectively blocked from the crater and the steam explosions diminished.

In April, fire fountains and lava flows became the dominant activity, forming a capping of hard, solid rocks over the lower slopes of Surtsey (Figure 13). The island was now as-

12   Black jets of ash explode to heights of 250 meters during the Surtsey eruption. Jet trails follow behind large volcanic bombs that whistle as they spin in flight. (Photograph by Thorleifur Einarsson.)

sured a place on the maps of the world; the waves still pounded on the shores but they met their match on the hardened lavas. The quiet effusion of lava continued for more than a year as Surtsey increased in area to 2.5 square kilometers, more than half capped by hard lava flows (Figure 14).

During 1965 and 1966, small explosive eruptions built low islands of volcanic debris both northeast and southwest

13   During 1964 Surtsey grew until the sea was blocked from the vent area. As a result, the eruption changed from explosions to incandescent lava fountains and flows. White steam clouds arising where the flows entered the sea replaced the black and gray explosion clouds. (Photograph by Captain Gardar Pálsson.)

of Surtsey, but these loose volcanic piles were not large or armored with lava flows and were soon washed away by oceanic storms.

In August 1966 renewed lava eruptions issued from the main crater on Surtsey. The lava flowed continuously in tunnels beneath its own crust to the edges of the island. We visited Surtsey during this last activity and were amazed to see that the orange tongues of lava pouring from the tunnels into the sea still glowed as they plunged beneath the waves. The insulating effects of the chilled skin and the steam layer on the surface of the lava were so effective that they prevented rapid quenching and steam explosions.

By June 1967 the eruption was over; it had lasted 3½ years. The total volume of volcanic ash and lava was slightly more than 1 cubic kilometer; only 9 percent of that was above sea level. The rates of eruption were highest in the early phases and diminished more or less continuously during the course of the activity. The lava temperatures on emission averaged about 1140°C.

The eruption had three main phases. First, there was the quiet, undetected underwater buildup from 130 meters below sea level to a few meters below sea level, possibly lasting several weeks. Second, explosive eruptions from shallow water built an island of loose volcanic debris. This was the beginning of the observable eruption. Third, the blocking of water from the vent stopped the explosions and allowed the quiet emission of lava flows (Figure 15).

The shape of Surtsey reflects the island's three-part volcanic history. The underwater base is steep-sided from the rapid cooling and piling up of the submarine lavas; the explosive debris forms steep crater walls and cones above sea level but has been cut into a flat bench at sea level by wave erosion; the final lava flows form gentle slopes where they poured out and hardened over the loose debris from earlier explosions.

Surtsey was born in sea, steam, and fire. Its rock ribs were molded by the environment into which it erupted. The Earth is shaped by such conflicting forces over immense spans of

A

14 Aerial photographs looking down vertically on the growing Island of Surtsey (about 1.3 kilometers in diameter when photographed). The light gray area is covered by volcanic ash and cinders. The dark areas in the south are basaltic lava flows extending into the sea, which cover the loose explosive debris and protect it from erosion by the waves. The dark area in the north is a lagoon. *A.* June 18, 1964. *B.* August 25, 1964. (Photographs by Landmaelingar Islands.)

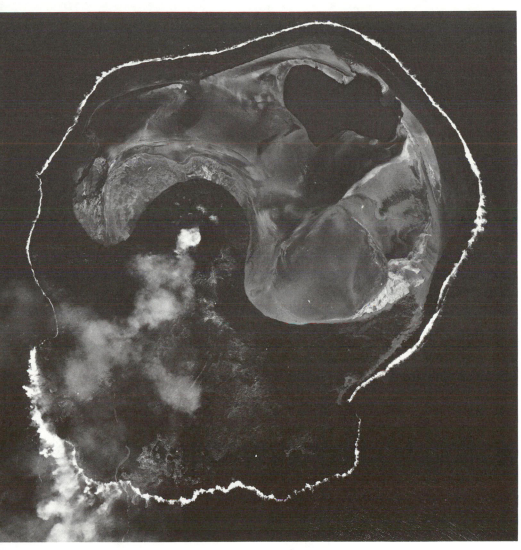

B

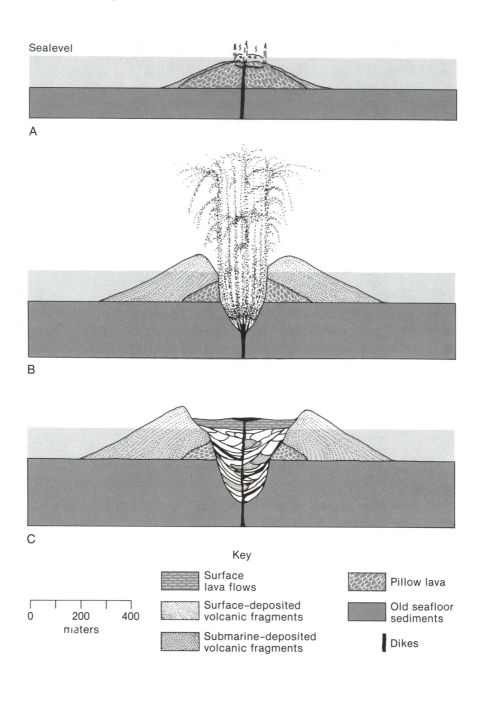

Sealevel

A

B

C

Key

Surface
lava flows

Surface-deposited
volcanic fragments

Submarine-deposited
volcanic fragments

Pillow lava

Old seafloor
sediments

Dikes

0   200   400
meters

15 Diagrammatic cross sections showing the three main phases of
the eruption of Surtsey: *A*. Submarine volcano of pillow lava is just
reaching the sea surface and becoming explosive. Pillow lava forms
during submarine eruptions where the pressure of overlying water
prevents explosive boiling. *B*. Continuous jetting explosions from
contact of seawater with erupting lava excavate the crater downward
into old seafloor sediments. *C*. Collapse of walls fills the deep crater
and these slumps are covered by surface flows of fluid basaltic lava.
These cross sections are schematic profiles drawn along a west
northwest–east southeast line through the center of the crater as
seen in Figure 14 A and B. Data on the deposits that slumped into
the deep crater (section *C*) were obtained by drilling. (Adapted from
J. G. Moore, *Geological Magazine* 122, 1985, p. 655.)

time. It is rare to witness these events condensed into less
than 4 years.

In one sense the story of Surtsey is just beginning. The new
island is closed to all but researchers studying the ways in
which, even in this hostile environment, life takes hold and
slowly but tenaciously develops a complex ecological system.

From empty sea, through chaos and barren island, to the
first touch of plants and insects, the story of Surtsey recapitu-
lates in a small way the origin of the Earth.

3

Fire Under the Sea

16 Hawaiian lava entering the sea. (Photograph by R. W. Grigg, University of Hawaii.)

*In nature things move violently to their place,
and calmly in their place.*

—FRANCIS BACON (1561–1626)

. . . .

What do Surtsey and other rift volcanoes tell us about the formation of the Earth? They tell us that the entire deep ocean floor, 60 percent of the Earth's surface, is of volcanic origin — the product of rift volcanism.

The worldwide rift system is 60,000 kilometers long, and nearly all of it is submarine. Where it does appear as land in places like Iceland, the Azores, and the Galapagos Islands, the volcanic activity is probably greater than along the submarine ridges; great enough, in fact, to build the ridge above sea level. The reason for this difference in volcanic activity is a topic of lively debate, and we'll return to it in Chapter 7, Hot Spots. However, most geologists now agree that the rift islands are reasonably typical of the volcanic and structural processes that occur on the mid-ocean ridges; they are certainly easier to study.

Geologists who have studied the ocean ridges believe that a reservoir of molten rock, known as a magma chamber, exists at a depth of only 1 or 2 kilometers beneath the central rift valley. This shallow body of molten rock is only a few kilometers wide and high, but it is tens of thousands of kilometers long, stretching along the crest of all the oceanic ridges. Molten rock from this chamber feeds up into the spreading rift and thus heals the crack between the separating plates (Figure 17).

The number of volcanic eruptions that occur every year to heal this submarine crack must be more than those recorded on land. Although a deep submarine volcanic eruption has

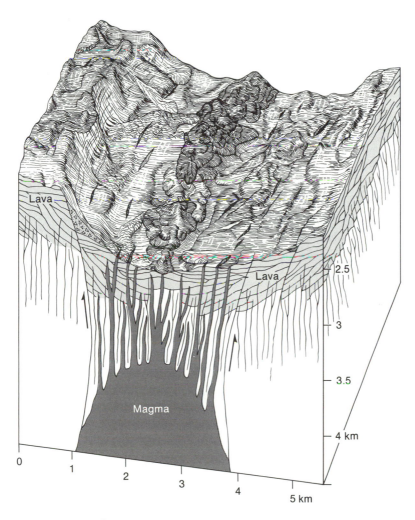

17 Diagram of the structure and submarine topography of the central rift valley of the Mid-Atlantic Ridge. The vertical scale is exaggerated two times. (After R. Hekinian, J. G. Moore, and W. B. Bryan, *Contributions to Mineralogy and Petrology* 58, 1976, p. 107.)

never been observed, a rough estimate of the number of such events can be made from the observed average of 1 eruption every 5 years in Iceland. Iceland represents about ¹⁄₂₀₀ of the length of the spreading oceanic ridges. To account for its extra elevation let's assume that Iceland's eruption rate is twice that of an equal length of the submarine ridges, whose volcanoes therefore erupt once every 10 years. Thus (200 Icelands) times (1/10 of an eruption per year) equals (20 eruptions per year) along the oceanic ridge system. The fact that not one of these deep submarine eruptions has ever been witnessed, even by oceanographic instruments, shows us that many frontiers remain to be crossed in our exploration of the Earth.

The volume of volcanic rock needed to heal the scar between the spreading plates is enormous. Every year 2.5 square kilometers of new seafloor is formed by the spreading of the plates. The rocky plates are 1 or 2 kilometers thick at their spreading edges. Hence the volume of new volcanic rock amounts to about 4 cubic kilometers of new oceanic crust formed every year.

The description of the Surtsey eruption in Chapter 2 contains an interesting paradox. The eruption of molten rock from a vent at shallow depth in the sea led to violent steam explosions. However, the lava that flowed through tunnels to the growing edge of Surtsey was seen to flow beneath the waves and to generate white steam clouds without violent disruption of the molten rock. Both were fire under the sea. Why was only the former explosive?

The answer involves the amount of water and other gases dissolved in the magma, which is normally about 0.5 percent of the weight of the molten rock. Magma from great depth erupted in shallow water quickly forms a chilled glassy rind. At the low surface pressures, most gases boil out of the molten rock and greatly expand in volume. This expansion fractures the glassy rind of the venting magma and allows seawater access to a large surface of finely broken but still hot rock. The steam generated by this contact water, added to the steam and other gases boiling out from within the magma, gives rise to the explosions.

Lava that has been erupted from a crater on land and has then moved through tunnels to the sea has already lost most of its dissolved gases. As it flows into the sea, it forms sacklike bodies of lava with chilled glassy rinds; these bodies are called *pillow lava* (Figure 18). The "pillows" do not fracture from the expansion of internal gases because those gases have already boiled away on land (Figure 16). A relatively small surface area loses heat to the surrounding water, and the quiet formation of steam takes place without explosions (Figure 19).

This process suggests that lavas emitted from vents in deep water, deep enough that the dissolved gases can't boil and expand, will also quietly form pillow lava. Because the contact water will be under too high pressure to boil, no steam will form. The violence of fire under the sea is thus controlled by depth. The common sense notion that fire and water are antagonistic originates in the limited view of our surface pressure environment. Of course the term *fire* is used loosely. In this context, fire means hot and glowing, not the combustion of a fuel with oxygen to produce flames.

The critical depth below which submarine lava is not explosive depends on the dissolved gas content and the temperature of the magma, but for all practical purposes this depth is only about 30 meters below sea level. Most of the oceanic ridges where the seafloor is spreading and new oceanic crust is forming are more than 2000 meters below sea level. Pillow lava thus forms much of the pavement of the spreading seafloors. Rocks dredged from the ridges by oceanographic ships and sampled on recent dives by scientists in special submersibles confirm this theory (Figure 20).

Jim Moore, one of the divers who descended 3000 meters into the valley along the crest of the Mid-Atlantic Ridge, describes the scene as a strange, silent land of pillow lava hills and yawning cracks, with a dusting of sedimentary mud. The pillow lava forms steep-sided hills 20 to 30 meters high and 0.5 to 1.0 kilometer wide near the center of the 4-kilometer-wide rift valley. These hills appear fresh and recently erupted; they clearly mark the very axis of the spreading oceanic ridge system.

On the valley floor on either side of the hills, many of the lavas look older. They are being covered with loose sedimentary debris that is slowly raining down from the ocean surface above. Most of the sediment is composed of microscopic

A

B

18   Pillow lava formed by volcanic flows under water compose some
of the most widespread rocks on Earth. *A.* Pillow lava formed
beneath the prehistoric glacial ice on Iceland. *B.* Young pillow lava
on the Mid-Atlantic Ridge 2700 meters below the ocean surface.
(Photograph taken from the submersible *Alvin* by W. B. Bryan of
Woods Hole Oceanographic Institution.)

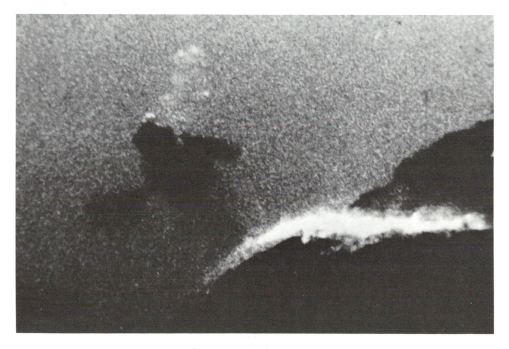

19   Diver studies the process of pillow-lava formation. The growing
pillow in the right foreground is enlarging along a red-hot seam
(white in this photograph). The lack of steam, even at this shallow
depth, indicates there is little conduction of heat from the molten
lava to the water. The lavas from Kilauea Volcano, Hawaii, entering
the sea in 1971 and 1973 provided diving geologists the first
opportunity to observe directly the formation of this widespread
type of rock. (Photograph by Lee Tepley from the movie *Fire Under
the Sea*, by Moonlight Productions, Mountain View, California.)

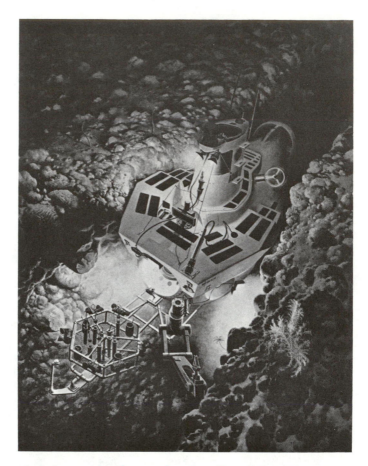

20 The submersible *Alvin* in the rift valley of the Mid-Atlantic Ridge. This artist's conception shows *Alvin* exploring an open fracture cutting across young pillow lava at a depth of 2600 meters. (Painting by the National Geographic Society.)

shells of calcium carbonate formed by floating plants and animals. The relative age of the submarine lava flows can be established by the thickness of the sedimentary mud that slowly accumulates with time (Figure 21).

Deep cracks parallel to the rift valley cut across the older lavas. These cracks result from the pulling apart of the entire

21 View down into an open fracture in the rift valley of the
Mid-Atlantic Ridge. The fracture cuts across sediment-covered pillow
lava and was evidently formed by the forces separating the plates.
This photo was taken at a depth of about 2700 meters during Project
FAMOUS (French–American Mid-Ocean Undersea Study) in 1974.
Similar above sea-level fractures cut through lava flows in the rift
zones of Iceland. (Photograph by W. B. Bryan, Woods Hole
Oceanographic Institution.)

ocean ridge system. The steep walls that form the sides of the
rift valley appear to be normal faults along which the valley
has dropped down 500 meters relative to the ridge.

For more than 1000 kilometers on either side of the rift
valley, the Mid-Atlantic Ridge slopes generally downward
away from the ridge over rugged and fractured volcanic terrain into deep basins 4000 to 5000 meters below sea level
(Figure 22).

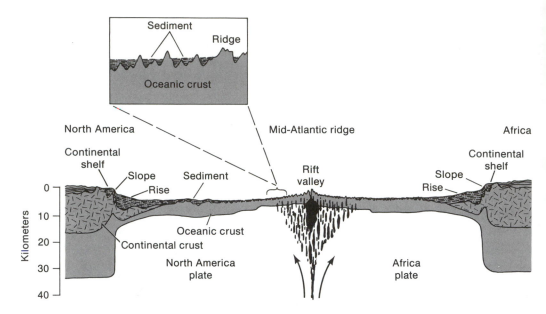

22 Cross section of the Earth beneath the Atlantic Ocean Basin. North America and Africa are both moving with the spreading seafloor, forming "passive" continental margins. Sediments accumulating in the valleys between the volcanic ridges slowly bury the rugged submarine mountains. (After B. C. Heezen, in F. Press and R. Siever, *Earth*, Second Edition, p. 262. W. H. Freeman and Company, Copyright © 1978.)

The East Pacific Rise spreads at a faster rate than does the Mid-Atlantic Ridge; its magnetic stripes indicate separation rates of 5 to 15 centimeters per year. Recent exploration of this rift system has revealed some interesting similarities and differences between Atlantic and Pacific seafloor spreading.

Exploratory dives in the submersible *Alvin*, operated by the Woods Hole Oceanographic Institution, were concentrated in an area just south of Baja California at 2500 meters depth. There the rift axis is only about 1 kilometer wide, and the spreading of the East Pacific Rise is 6 centimeters per year—about three times the spreading rate of the Mid-Atlantic Ridge.

Besides young pillow lava, some smooth-surfaced basaltic lava flows and solidified lava lakes were encountered. A fractured zone with fissures generally parallel to the rift system extends ½ to 2 kilometers on each side of the youngest lavas. Major fault scarps as much as 70 meters high facing in toward the rift axis extend outward from the spreading center (Figure 23). The locations of earthquakes and sea-bottom evidence of active faulting stop about 10 kilometers out,

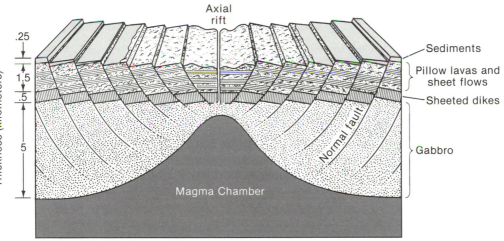

23   Schematic cross section of a spreading mid-ocean ridge. Active submarine volcanism is concentrated within a narrow area along the rift axis. Faulting forms the down-dropped blocks of older volcanic rock on both sides of the spreading axis. The magma forms as the plates diverge and mantle rock rises and melts with the decrease of pressure. It collects in a chamber below the spreading center. Along the borders of the magma chamber a coarse-crystalline rock of basaltic composition called gabbro is formed. At the top of the chamber the magma rises as the plates diverge and cools as vertical dikes. At the surface lava flows out and hardens in the form of sheets and pillows. As the new crust moves away from the spreading center, a layer of sediments is deposited on it. The mature crust has a layered structure from the top down: sediments, sheet and pillow lavas, dikes, and gabbros. (From Jean Francheteau, "The Oceanic Crust. East Pacific Rise." Copyright © 1983 by Scientific American, Inc. All rights reserved.)

indicating that active spreading is concentrated across a 20-kilometer-wide zone, mostly in the central axis. Beyond this zone, the plates continue to move passively away on their long journey beneath the Pacific Ocean.

Submarine hot springs were also found on this expedition. Exotic life forms and metal sulfide deposits associated with these hydrothermal vents are among the most exciting geological discoveries of the past decade. Warm springs (20°C) were first observed during dives on the Galapagos Ridge in 1977, and in 1979 extremely hot springs (350°C) were observed during dives at 21° North Latitude on the East Pacific Rise. Bruce Luyendyk of the University of California at Santa Barbara was one of the scientists on the discovery dives, and his own words best describe the experience.

> The scene was like one out of an old horror movie. Shimmering water rose between the basaltic pillows along the axis of the neovolcanic zone. Large white clams as much as 30 centimeters long nestled between the black pillows, while crabs scampered blindly across the volcanic terrain. Most dramatic of all were the clusters of giant tube worms, some of them as long as 3 meters.

On a subsequent dive the scientific submariners found another impressive sight: ". . . extremely hot fluids, blackened by sulfide precipitates, were blasting upward through chimneylike vents as much as 10 meters tall and 40 centimeters wide. We named the vents 'black smokers'" (Figure 24 and Color Plate 26).

In the years since, other undersea expeditions have found these strange oases of life and sulfide metal deposits at scattered places along the axes of spreading rifts in the Atlantic and North Pacific oceans. They are probably common but not continuous features of the entire world rift system.

The basic significance of these strange colonies of life on the dark seafloor and their associated mineral deposits is just beginning to be appreciated fully by biologists and geologists. The bacteria that feed the food chain of strange worms,

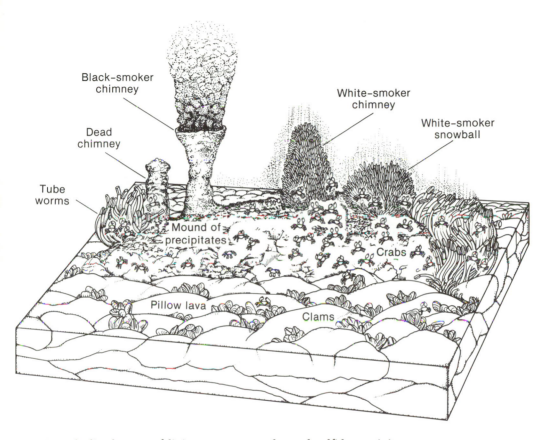

Black-smoker
chimney

White-smoker
chimney

White-smoker
snowball

Dead
chimney

Tube
worms

Mound of
precipitates

Crabs

Pillow lava

Clams

24 Idealized scene of living creatures and metal sulfide precipitates
at a submarine hot spring 2500 meters deep along the rift zone of
the East Pacific Rise. The white-smoker chimney is made of burrows
of Pompeii worms. White, cloudy fluids emitted by the white
smokers have temperatures up to 300°C. The hottest water, up to
350°C, pours from the black smoker and precipitates a dark cloud of
metal sulfide particles as it is cooled by the surrounding seawater.
(From K. C. Macdonald and B. P. Luyendyk, "The Crest of the East
Pacific Rise." Copyright © 1981 by Scientific American, Inc. All
rights reserved.)

clams, and crabs live on volcanic heat, hydrogen sulfide, and
oxygen; sunlight is not needed (Figure 25). Until the last few
years, the sun and photosynthesis were considered the only
basic suppliers of energy to life on Earth.

25   Tube worms and other unusual life forms flourish near submarine hot springs. This photograph shows clusters of large tube worms, some as long as 2 meters, waving in warm water at the margins of high temperature vents. Chemosynthetic bacteria form the base of this sunless food chain that also supports clams and crabs. (Photograph taken at 21° North Latitude on the East Pacific Rise during the RISE Expedition, F. N. Speiss, Scripps Institution of Oceanography, 1979, and provided by William Normark, U.S. Geological Survey.)

The metallic sulfide deposits are of equal importance; they precipitate as seawater chills the submarine hot springs, forming mounds and crusts rich in iron, copper, and zinc. As the seafloor separates, these deposits are spread into extensive layers of potentially great economic value (more on this in Chapter 13).

One of the main arguments about rift volcanoes is whether they are a cause or an effect of the rifting apart of the oceanic ridges. Does the intrusion of volcanic rocks push apart the plates, or does the pulling or dragging apart of the plates form cracks through which the magma can rise to the surface?

Most experts now favor the latter view, although the answer may be both.

During the last 20 years we have been measuring the spreading in Iceland with sensitive surveying instruments that can detect changes of less than 1 centimeter over distances of 5 kilometers. The results of this study indicate that the rift zones slowly widen and sink a few millimeters per year across distances of 10 to 30 kilometers, without earthquakes or volcanic eruptions. When the tensional strain reaches the breaking point, the rift fractures (Figure 26).

A rifting event takes place in a few hours or days. Open cracks form parallel to the rift, earthquake swarms jolt the local area, and lava erupts from some of the fissures.

26 Aerial photograph of fractures in the rift zone of Iceland. These fractures mark the continuation of the crest of the Mid-Atlantic Ridge across Iceland. The lava flows in this area are less than 6000 years old. Summer homes dot the edge of the lake formed by the central valley of the rift.

We were lucky enough to be in northern Iceland when one of these rifting episodes occurred on September 7, 1977. An earthquake swarm at Krafla Volcano was followed in rapid succession by a brief but spectacular volcanic fissure eruption and ground cracking parallel to the rift. In a zone about 2 kilometers across and 20 kilometers long, the cracking formed open fractures up to 20 centimeters wide with vertical offsets as large as 1 meter. All this occurred between 3:00 P.M. and midnight (Figure 27).

One of the cracks cut through a producing geothermal steam field. Some magma must have been injected along this fracture, for one of the steam wells erupted brief spurts of incandescent lava. The erupting lava cut through the heavy metal pipe at the well head and showered a few tons of frothy lava fragments around the well. This is the only known case where lava has erupted from a man-made vent (Figure 28).

One survey line about 4 kilometers long that crossed the fracture zone lengthened more than 1 meter. Survey lines on the flanks of the new fracture zone showed contraction. The picture of rifting that emerges is one of slow stretching for 100 to 200 years over a wide zone, followed by rupture that concentrates the deformation into a narrow central zone and allows the flanks to contract back to an unstretched condition. It's like pulling a rubber band slowly and then cutting it in the middle; all the stretching that had slowly accumulated is suddenly concentrated in the cut, and the sides contract. Perhaps a sudden tear in a piece of elastic cloth when it is slowly stretched would be a better analogy since its dimensions fit the plates more closely than does a rubber band.

The length of the tear in a rifting episode is 10 to 100 kilometers long, only a very small fraction of the length of the entire rift system. The rifting episodes are infrequent in any one place, perhaps only once every few hundred years.

27   A gaping fracture formed during an earthquake swarm in northern Iceland on September 7, 1977. This rifting event was related to an eruption of Krafla Volcano. The cone in the background was formed in a prehistoric eruption of Krafla.

28 Incandescent lava was briefly ejected from this geothermal steam well in Iceland during the eruption of Krafla Volcano on September 7, 1977. A fracture somewhere between the surface and the 1200-meter depth of the well broke the well casing and allowed a small amount of molten rock to enter the producing well. The steam lifted the magma spray to the surface where it melted and abraded its way through the pipe. The few tons of small lava bombs that were ejected form the granular surface material. This is the only known case of a volcanic vent produced by drilling.

However, at any given time somewhere over the entire length of the ocean ridge system rifting is probably occurring.

The presence of magma under pressure beneath the rift zones probably aids the rupture process just as a wedge speeds the felling of a leaning tree. The processes of rifting and volcanism are so interrelated that it is difficult to sort out cause and effect — reminding us of Samuel Butler's remark that "a hen is just an egg's way of making another egg."

There is no doubt, however, that great chains of volcanoes, mostly submarine, circle the Earth in several belts along the crests of the oceanic ridges. They owe their origin to the still mysterious forces that spread the plates. Surtsey is only a visible tip of this vast hidden activity.

4
Mount St. Helens

29 Five smaller explosive eruptions occurred during the summer and fall following the giant May 18, 1980, eruption of Mount St. Helens. This ash cloud on July 22 churned upward to an altitude of 18 kilometers in just 8 minutes. (Photograph by Katia Krafft.)

A natural calamity will strike at about the time the terror of the last one is forgotten.

—JAPANESE PROVERB

. . . .

T he violent eruption of Washington State's Mount St. Helens in May 1980 was one of the world's most closely monitored — and most fully documented — volcanic events (Figure 30). Volcanologists had been watching with keen interest, alerted by 2 months of mild but ominous activity that signaled the awakening of the sleeping mountain (Figure 31).

At 8:32 A.M. on May 18, Mount St. Helens was shaken by a magnitude 5 earthquake, centered 1 to 2 kilometers beneath the north flank. Geologists Keith and Dorothy Stoffel, flying in a light plane about 400 meters above the summit at just that moment, saw several small ice falls start within the steep crater. About 15 seconds later they were the closest witnesses to the onset of one of the largest landslides in history, followed by a huge volcanic eruption.

"The whole north side of the summit crater began to move instantaneously as one gigantic mass. The nature of movement was eerie; not like anything we'd ever seen before," Dorothy recalled. "The entire mass began to ripple and churn without moving laterally. Then the whole north side of the summit started moving to the north along a deep-seated slide plane" (Figure 32 top).

Seconds later, a massive explosion shook the mountain. From the Stoffels' viewpoint the initial explosion cloud seemed to mushroom sideways to the north and plunge down the slope, but in the plane they neither felt nor heard the

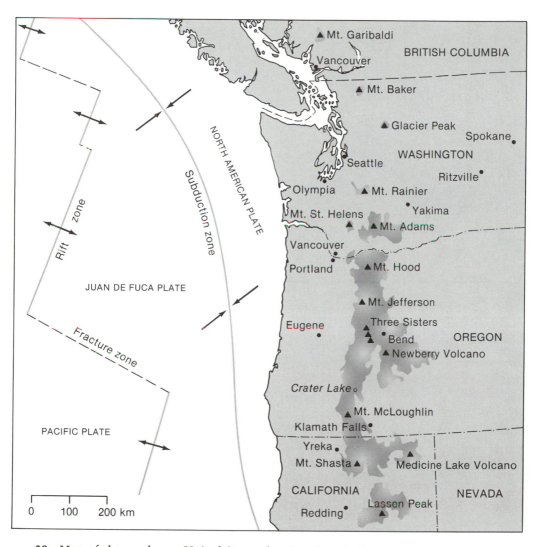

30 Map of the northwest United States showing Cascade Range volcanoes and their relationship to the subduction of the Juan de Fuca plate beneath the North America plate. Submarine volcanoes and hot springs have recently been discovered along the rift zone that forms the west edge of the Juan de Fuca plate. Dark gray areas are volcanic rocks less than 2 million years old. (Data from the U.S. Geological Survey.)

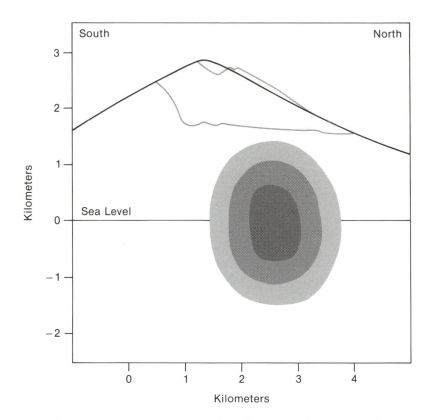

31 Cross section of Mount St. Helens illustrates changes associated with the great 1980 eruption. Solid line at top shows surface as of 1979. Upper broken line shows the crater and bulge that developed between late March and early May 1980. The shaded area indicates the region in which the thousands of earthquakes that accompanied the growing bulge occurred. The darker the shading, the higher the density of earthquake locations. Lower broken line shows the crater after the May 18 eruption. (Data from U.S. Geological Survey and University of Washington Department of Geophysics.)

explosion (Figure 32 bottom). Realizing the enormous size of the eruption, survival became their first concern. They dove at full throttle to gain speed, but the expanding cloud appeared to be gaining on them; by turning south they finally outran it. Behind them the rapidly growing ash clouds thrust north and northwest. To the east the clouds rose into billowing mushroom shapes with heavy ashfall, and lightning bolts thousands of meters high shot through the clouds (Figure 33). Half an hour later the Stoffels, shaken but safe, landed at Portland airport.

In the avalanche they had witnessed from the air, nearly 3 cubic kilometers of crushed rock and glacier ice plunged down into Spirit Lake and the North Fork of the Toutle River. Exploding steam helped to fluidize the avalanche, and it accelerated rapidly to velocities of 250 kilometers per hour. One lobe of the gigantic mass plowed through the west arm of Spirit Lake and into the valley to the north of the lake. The momentum of another lobe carried it over a ridge 360 meters above the floor of the valley it had just swept across, but the bulk of the fluidized debris funneled down the valley of the Toutle for 21 kilometers, forming a hummocky deposit 1 to 2 kilometers wide and up to 200 meters thick (Figure 34).

Superheated groundwater flashed to steam as the great avalanche of rock and ice suddenly released the pressure in the volcanic edifice. At the same time, dissolved gases began exploding from the shallow magma body that had recently pushed up into Mount St. Helens. The steam blast, magma explosion, and giant avalanche combined to form a lateral blast of dense, debris-filled steam clouds as hot as 300°C, surging northward from the breached volcano at speeds of 100 to 400 kilometers per hour. This steam blast and its fluidized charge of volcanic rock fragments devastated more than 500 square kilometers of mountainous terrain northwest, north, and northeast of Mount St. Helens. The ground-hugging black clouds rolled over four major ridges and valleys, reaching as far as 28 kilometers from their source.

The destruction was complete. For the first few kilometers entire trees as large as 1 to 2 meters in diameter were uprooted and swept away with the roiling explosion cloud. Beyond this was a blowdown zone 10 to 15 kilometers wide where prime Douglas Firs were snapped off like matchsticks

(Figure 35). At the outer limits of destruction, trees were still standing but their needles were scorched beyond recovery.

The blowdown zone looked as if a great shock wave or concussion front had knocked the trees down in a pattern radial to the exploding peak, but the evidence showed that that was not what had happened. Survivors near the edge of the devastated area heard only a moderately loud explosion or roaring sound 2 to 3 minutes before the black cloud with its hot hurricane winds descended upon them. The average velocity of the growing front of the steam blast clouds was below the speed of sound. On closer inspection, the pattern of downed trees showed turbulent eddies and curving streamlines. Near the edge of the devastated area most trees were blown down in down-valley directions, even turning toward the source of the surging clouds (Figure 36).

Gravity apparently provided energy to the dense, fluidized mass as the initial steam blast energy waned. As the turbulent internal winds abated, ash and rock debris from the dense clouds settled to the surface in deposits that ranged in thickness from about 1 meter to a few millimeters. Angular fragments of old volcanic rocks and fresh, hot dacite were carried in the blast clouds as far as 15 kilometers from the exploding peak. Trees were charred and blackened on the blast side out

32 A remarkable sequence of photographs of the explosion of Mount St. Helens was taken by Keith Ronnholm, a geophysicist from Seattle, Washington, on the morning of May 18, 1980. He was camped near Bear Meadows, 18 kilometers northeast of the peak. After taking the pictures Ronnholm was enveloped in the blackout of heavy ash and pumice fall, but he was just beyond the area of total devastation. The top photograph, taken 40 seconds after the great avalanche began, shows the huge landslide blocks being overtopped by the subsequent explosion. The bottom photograph, taken 20 seconds later, shows the rapidly-growing explosion cloud thrusting northward from Mount St. Helens. (Photographs by Keith Ronnholm, © 1980.)

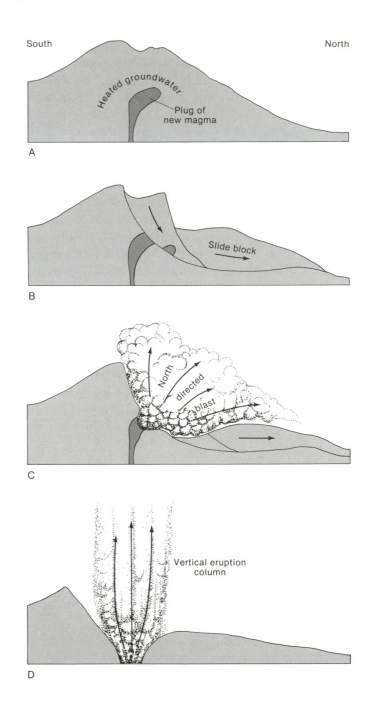

South   North

Heated groundwater

Plug of
new magma

A

Slide block

B

North
directed
blast

C

Vertical eruption
column

D

to 7 kilometers on the northwest and north, and as far as 18 kilometers on the northeast flank of Mount St. Helens.

The worst was over in the first 10 minutes but the vertical eruption column roared on, reaching more than 16 kilometers in altitude for much of the day. The source of this almost-continuous exploding and uprushing column of gas and ash was the effervescing shallow magma body being progressively cored out to greater and greater depths. The abrasive uprush continued to enlarge the horseshoe-shaped crater that was initially formed by the avalanche and lateral blasts.

High-altitude winds blew all day to the northeast, and ash began falling on central Washington towns by midmorning. At Yakima (150 kilometers distant) the first ashfall was a sand-sized "salt and pepper" layer composed of dark rock fragments and lighter colored feldspar crystal fragments, overlain by a thicker silt-sized layer of volcanic glass particles. Thirty kilometers north of Yakima the maximum ashfall was about 20 millimeters. Eastward the fine ash thickened, reaching more than 70 millimeters near Ritzville, Washington, 330 kilometers from Mount St. Helens. Here the texture was like talcum powder. Though the ash thinned to 5 millimeters near Spokane, 430 kilometers northeast of the volcano, visibility was still reduced to 3 meters in near-darkness

33 Schematic cross sections of Mount St. Helens showing early stages of the May 18, 1980, eruption: A. Shallow plug of magma injected beneath the volcano caused the high north face to bulge outward, and has heated the groundwater. Minor explosions of heated groundwater have excavated a small summit crater. B. Magnitude 5 earthquake caused by the continuing injection of the magma plug shakes loose the oversteepened north flank of the mountain into two or more massive slide blocks. C. As the superheated groundwater and magma plug are suddenly depressurized, they explode into a huge steam blast that sweeps northward for many kilometers. D. After avalanche and blast have exposed the main magma conduit, gases dissolved in the magma continue to boil out in continuous vertical jetting explosions. (Modified from J. G. Moore and W. C. Albee, 1981, U.S. Geological Survey Professional Paper 1250, p. 132.)

34 View to the east showing Mount St. Helens and the huge avalanche deposit in the valley of the North Fork of the Toutle River. (U.S. Geological Survey photograph by R. M. Krimmel, June 30, 1980.)

35 Trees blown down by the hot, debris-filled hurricane winds in the Mount St. Helens steam blast cloud fell into streamlined rows over hundreds of square kilometers. These logs are large Douglas Firs and other conifers 1 to 2 meters in diameter and 40 to 60 meters long. (Photograph by Katia Krafft.)

by 3:00 P.M. A trace of ash fell on Denver about noon on May 19; the ash cloud crossed the United States within 3 days.

Mudflows were another major aspect of the eruption. These flows consisted of a slurry of volcanic ash and fine rock particles mixed with water, and had the consistency of wet cement. The ash blanket near the mountain and the crushed rock in the avalanche deposit provided the solid matter; the extra water probably derived from several sources — melting snow and ice, the water displaced from Spirit Lake and the North Fork of the Toutle River, water from the compaction and settling of the saturated avalanche deposits, and condensing steam.

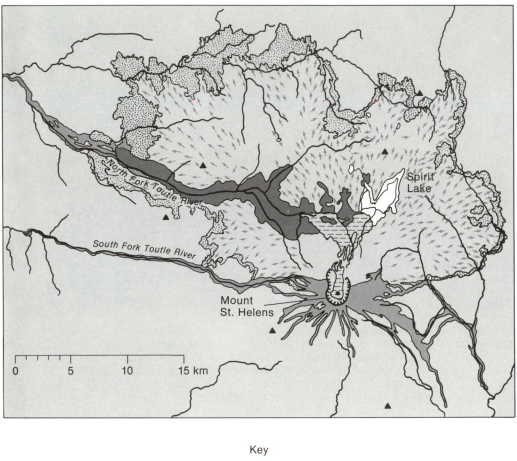

Key

 Lava dome

 Pyroclastic flow deposits

Mudflow deposits and
scoured areas

 Scorch zone

 Down–timber; arrows indicate
direction of tree blowdown

Debris-avalanche deposits

▲ Mountain summits

36 Map of the region surrounding Mount St. Helens showing
effects of the May 18, 1980, eruption and the subsequent lava dome.
The devastated area is more than 500 square kilometers. The size of
Spirit Lake was increased by the eruption; both the old and the new
shorelines are shown. (Adapted from U.S. Geological Survey.)

The highest flood crest in the North Fork of the Toutle River arrived at the gauging station that evening and destroyed the station. High mudflow marks on trees indicate a floodstage of 16 meters, 9 meters higher than any flood previously recorded on the Toutle River. Downstream, mudflow deposits clogged the channels of the Cowlitz River and caused severe shoaling of the navigation channel in the Columbia River.

Sometime after the initial avalanche and steam blast eruption, pyroclastic flows of fine ash and pumice blocks began rushing down the north slope of Mount St. Helens through the breach in the newly formed crater (Figures 37 and 38). These fluidized emulsions of hot (though not molten) rock fragments and volcanic gases formed dense flows that issued from the crater beneath the ascending ash cloud. Successive flows churned down the north slope at speeds up to 100 kilometers per hour, covering the earlier landslide and blast deposits, and reaching the south edge of Spirit Lake. Contact with water by these hot pyroclastic flows caused secondary explosions, sending steam and ash clouds 2 kilometers high.

The total disaster was staggering: 57 people killed and more than $1 billion in loss and damage — mostly to the lumber industry. Perhaps the greatest damage was psychological; in the northwest United States the image of the Cascade volcanoes had changed from silent guardian peaks to potential killers.

Although the suddenness, complexity, and scale of the May 18 eruption were not anticipated, the fact that a major eruption occurred was not a complete surprise. In 1978 Dwight Crandell and Donal Mullineaux of the U.S. Geological Survey had issued a report about Mount St. Helens that concluded with the warning, ". . . an eruption is more likely to occur within the next 100 years, and perhaps even before the end of this century."

This forecast was based on their studies of the character, distribution, and ages of prehistoric eruption deposits from the volcano, as well as scattered accounts by explorers about eruptions that had occurred at Mount St. Helens between

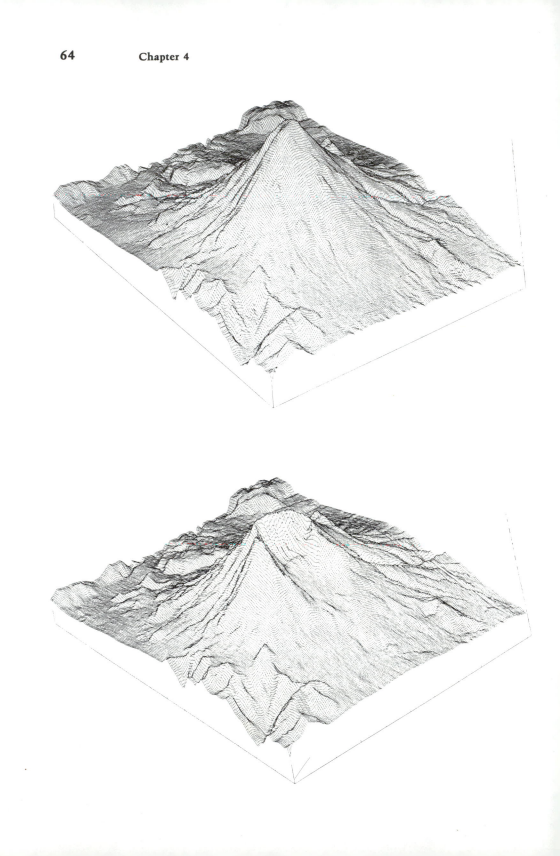

1831 and 1857. Just 2 years after their report was published, the quiet interval ended.

Beginning on March 20, 1980, a swarm of small to moderate earthquakes centered beneath Mount St. Helens announced the volcano's awakening. A seismograph had already been placed on the west flank by University of Washington seismologists, and soon after the swarm started additional seismographs were installed to record and locate the earthquakes more precisely. On March 25, 47 earthquakes of magnitude 3 or more occurred within a 12-hour period at shallow depths under the volcano's north flank.

The first eruptive activity — small explosions of steam — began 2 days later, forming a new crater about 70 meters wide on the snow-and-ice-covered summit. Large east-west cracks also developed across the summit area. A second small crater formed on March 29, and blue flames — possibly burning hydrogen sulfide gas — were visible from the air at night. The next day, 93 small eruptions of steam and ash were observed.

On April 1 the seismographs recorded the first volcanic tremor, a more or less continuous ground vibration observed at many active volcanoes. The precise cause of volcanic tremor is not clear, but it presumably reflects the movement of magma or the rumbling formation and collapse of subsurface gas bubbles associated with incipient boiling of groundwater or gases dissolved in magma.

The small steam and ash explosions continued — some as single explosions, others as pulsating jets lasting for hours. Columns of gas and ash climbed to 3 kilometers above the summit. The craters grew into a single oval pit 500 meters by

37 Computer-graphic models of Mount St. Helens before and after May 18, 1980. The avalanche and eruption removed the top 400 meters of the peak, forming a breached crater 2 kilometers wide, 4 kilometers long, and 700 kilometers deep. These views are from the northeast, and exaggerate the relief. (Created by the U.S. Geological Survey and Dynamic Graphics, Inc.)

300 meters across and 200 meters deep. The ash consisted of fragments of old volcanic rock, and the gas emissions were largely steam mixed with carbon dioxide, sulfur dioxide, hydrogen sulfide, and hydrogen chloride. The small explosive eruptions during this period apparently resulted from groundwater high in the volcanic cone being heated above its subsurface boiling point and flashing suddenly into steam, much as a geyser does, but with energy enough to tear loose rock fragments and blast out a crater.

As the high level of seismic activity continued — about 50 earthquakes of magnitude 3 or greater per day — another ominous sign became apparent. Scientists comparing aerial photographs taken before and after the beginning of activity noticed major deformation high on the north flank of the cone. Careful measurements showed that a bulge was growing upward and outward, causing a spreading network of large cracks in the cover of snow and ice. Maps made by the U.S. Geological Survey from aerial photographs taken on April 12 disclosed that the bulge was 2 kilometers in diameter and had already moved up and out by as much as 100 meters.

Repeated ground surveys made in late April and early May established that the bulge continued to expand northward at a rate of about 1.5 meters per day. This rapidly deforming area was directly over the center of the earthquake zone 2 kilometers below. Scientists on the site agreed that the continuing seismic swarm and surface bulging were an indication that magma was being injected at a shallow depth beneath Mount St. Helens. They concluded that if the intrusion

38   Before and after views of Mount St. Helens. The photograph at the top was taken in June 1970; the one at the bottom in May, 1980. The pre-1980 summit elevation was 2950 meters, the cone rising from a base with an elevation of about 1000 meters. The rim of the post-eruption crater has elevations ranging from 2400 to 2550 meters, and the crater floor elevation varies from 1800 to 1900 meters. (1980 photograph by Ross Hamilton, U.S. Geological Survey.)

of magma continued at this high rate, a significant eruption was likely; the major questions were how soon it might occur, and how violent it might be.

Small steam and ash explosions continued through the first half of May, and the rate of seismic and deformation activity continued unabated. On May 15, 16, and 17 there were no eruptions, and although the earthquakes and bulging continued, their rates showed no change. May 18 dawned a beautiful spring day, but at 8:32 A.M. the scientists' worst fears became a reality.

Among the dead and missing that day was David Johnston, a U.S. Geological Survey scientist who was measuring the growing bulge from a ridge 10 kilometers north of the volcano's summit. The scale of the eruption was unexpectedly large, especially the great area devastated by the lateral blast, which was unprecedented in the prehistoric eruption record of Mount St. Helens. The suddenness with which the avalanche broke open the hot groundwater and magma system beneath the summit of the volcano caused much of the violence. Had the unroofing of the shallow magma injection occurred in a slower, more piecemeal way — for example, in a series of increasingly larger explosions over a period of several days — the area devastated by the eruption would have been much smaller.

On five more occasions through the summer and early fall of 1980 smaller explosive eruptions of Mount St. Helens generated ash clouds and pyroclastic flows (Figure 29 and Color Plate 17). During two eruptive episodes domes of viscous lava were pushed up over the vent area in the crater, but then were blown out by explosions. However, since October of that year a large lava dome has been episodically squeezing up over the vent area, and at this time (1989) it is 1 kilometer in diameter and 250 meters high (Figure 39). The episodes of rapid dome growth typically have lasted for several days, separated by quiet intervals of a few months to several years.

These dome growth episodes are preceded by several days of increasing seismic activity and increasing rates of ground deformation at the margins of the dome. Predictions of the

39 From 1981 to 1986 (and possibly continuing) a dome of viscous lava has intermittently squeezed up from the vent at Mount St. Helens. Seventeen episodes of dome growth, generally lasting from 1 to 3 weeks have built this 1-kilometer-wide, 250-meter-high dome of dacitic lava. More viscous than basalt, this high-silica lava has piled up over its vent. (U.S. Geological Survey photograph by Lyn Topinka, 1984.)

onset of rapid dome growth based on this continuous seismic and deformation monitoring have been excellent. Because the amount of growth in each episode has been roughly proportional to the length of the quiet interval that preceded it, the amount of lava in each episode has also been predictable.

The last episode of dome growth occurred during October 1986. If the trend of lava production being proportional to the quiet interval persists, then the next episode should be quite large. However, the general rate of magma reaching the surface and near surface at Mount St. Helens has been decreasing since the May 1980 eruption. This trend is also reflected in the generally decreasing amount of seismic activity. Unless there is a change in these waning trends, the present eruptive period of Mount St. Helens may be drawing to a close.

Even so, the danger of another explosion that could blow out part or all of the lava dome has not entirely disappeared. The sides of the lava dome are steep and unstable, and an avalanche of the dome's flank could suddenly unload the core of the still-hot dome, triggering an explosive eruption. Because the dome is much smaller than the pre-1980 summit of Mount St. Helens, and since its exposure to the surface allows much of its internal gases to escape, such an explosion, if it did occur, would probably be small in scale compared to the May 1980 eruption.

Mount St. Helens is one of 15 major volcanoes of the Cascade Range that extends from northern California into western Canada. Although each of these volcanoes is potentially active, only one other — Lassen Peak in California — has erupted in this century. The 63-year repose between the 1914–1917 Lassen eruptions and the 1980 (and continuing) eruption of Mount St. Helens was long enough for most Americans to forget that the Cascade Range is still alive and dangerous; after May 18, 1980, everyone remembered.

5

Ring of Fire

40   Cerro Negro Volcano, Nicaragua, 1968.

Far away, shrouded in fog we saw
the silhouettes of the volcanic islands—
links in Pluto's mighty chain.

—Y. MARKHININ (1971)

. . . .

Amerika is drifting away from Europe, but it is also drifting toward Japan. In fact, all the plates around the Pacific are slowly converging along subduction zones that encircle this vast ocean. Volcanoes related to these converging plate margins form a Ring of Fire that nearly surrounds the Pacific Basin (Figure 41).

Mount St. Helens and the other volcanoes of the Cascade Range are located on the subduction zone between the small Juan de Fuca plate and the North American plate. Volcanoes in Mexico, Central America, the Andes, New Zealand, Papua New Guinea, the Philippines, Japan, Kamchatka, and Alaska complete the circuit.

Subduction zones generate about 400 of the more than 500 known active volcanoes in the world; that is, those that have erupted at least once in historic time. The Mediterranean volcanoes of Italy and Greece are included in this tally.

There are major differences between subduction volcanoes and rift volcanoes. Subduction volcanoes form island arcs and high mountain chains rather than submarine ridges; they are more explosive and produce large volumes of ash as well as lava flows; their products are more variable in composition; even their basic shapes as individual mountains differ from those formed at extensional margins.

Rift volcanoes are located at the exact edges of the separating plates. In contrast, subduction volcanoes occur about 100

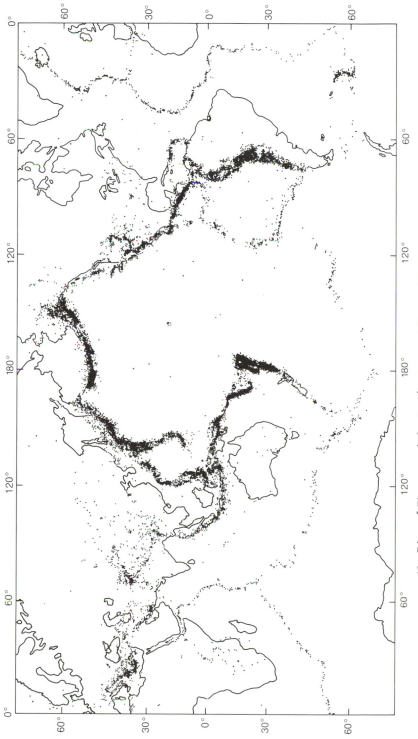

41 Ring of Fire around the Pacific Ocean, delineated by locations of earthquakes occurring between 1963 and 1977 with a magnitude greater than 4.5, as determined by the U.S. Geological Survey's National Earthquake Information Service. (Map plotted by the Environmental Data and Information Service of the National Oceanic and Atmospheric Administration.)

to 200 kilometers landward from the deep ocean trenches that mark the compressional edges of converging plates.

Chains of subduction volcanoes form graceful arcs a few thousand kilometers in length across the globe. A close look shows that 5 or 10 volcanoes often are in a fairly straight line a few hundred kilometers in length, with a slight bend or offset between adjoining groups. The bends between the groups form the overall arc, which is generally convex toward the open ocean side.

Japan is a good example of a subduction chain, with about 50 volcanoes along parts of 4 arcs. The deep-sea trenches lie 200 kilometers on the Pacific Ocean side of the volcanoes and mark the actual boundary between plates. A region of earthquakes dips from near the Earth's surface at the trenches beneath the island arcs. This region roughly outlines the upper surface of the Pacific and Philippine plates as they plunge beneath Asia.

The belt of volcanoes occurs on the overlying plate where the earthquake zone is 100 to 200 kilometers beneath the Earth's surface (Figure 42). Most of the large volcanoes are on

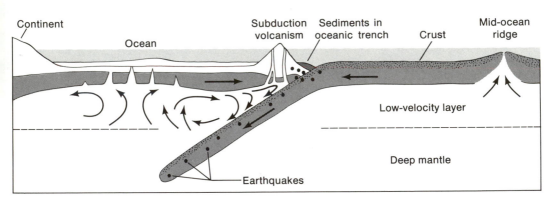

42 Plate of crust and solid upper mantle formed at the mid-ocean ridge moves on the plastic low-velocity layer and is thrust beneath a converging plate at a subduction zone. An oceanic trench forms where the plates converge, and an island arc of compressed rocks and volcanoes forms over the downgoing plate. (From M. Nafi Toksoz, "The Subduction of the Lithosphere." Copyright © 1975 by Scientific American, Inc. All rights reserved.)

the eastern edge of this belt where the earthquake zone is shallower. Japanese geologists refer to this eastern edge as the volcanic front. The number of volcanoes and their production of volcanic rocks decreases gradually with distance away from the volcanic front, toward Asia, but stops abruptly on the Pacific side of the volcanic front.

This setting is generally characteristic of all subduction zone volcanoes, and indicates that magma is being generated when the descending plate sinks to a depth of 100 to 200 kilometers. At one time geologists believed that the friction of the converging plates generated heat, and that this extra heat helped to melt the magma for subduction volcanoes. However, computer models of the temperatures beneath subduction zones show that the underthrusting plate carries some of its lower surface temperature down with it, in effect cooling part of the region deep beneath the volcanic front. Most geologists now consider that magma generated in subduction zones may be formed by the fluxing action of water and carbon dioxide in the oceanic sediments dragged down on the top of the underthrusting plate. Water, carbon dioxide, and minerals containing sodium and potassium lower the melting temperature of magma. Existing temperatures in the low-velocity layer at 100 to 200 kilometer depth along the top of the subducting plate are high enough to produce this lower-melting temperature magma. Addition of water and carbon dioxide would also increase the magma's gas content and explain the greater explosiveness of subduction volcanoes.

Once enough magma has formed at sufficient depth, the greater density of the surrounding rocks exerts an upward force on the magma. Its ascent toward the surface may be aided by fractures in the overlying plate. The distance between volcanoes in island arcs is usually about 50 to 70 kilometers. This spacing is about the thickness of the overlying plate, which is reasonable because the spacing of fractures in a rigid plate resting on a soft layer tends to be about the same as the thickness of the plate.

The silica content of most rift volcanoes is about 50 percent and varies only a few percentage points, while the silica content of subduction volcanoes varies from about 50 to 70 percent. The silica content largely determines which minerals form in volcanic rocks and thereby controls the nature of the mineral deposits and sediments associated with the volcanic rocks. For example, the mineral quartz (SiO_2) does not form until the silica content of rocks exceeds 55 percent. In Iceland there is no quartz in the basaltic lavas; there are no white, sandy beaches with quartz grains; and there are no quartz veins containing precious metal deposits. On the Ring of Fire, however, the volcanic rocks usually contain quartz grains that erode to form quartz sand beaches; and gold, silver, and copper mines pock the eroded stumps of older volcanoes.

The composition of volcanic rocks is controlled by three major factors: partial melting processes; partial crystallization processes, and contamination by surrounding rocks.

Partial melting is the process by which part of the solid upper mantle of the Earth is turned into magma. Rocks are a mixture of several chemical compounds, and these do not all have the same melting points. In a partial melt, the first fraction to melt will have a larger proportion of the low-melting-point compounds than the parent rock. An analogy is the extraction of alcohol from hard cider by freezing and thawing. If a completely frozen block of hard cider is slowly melted, the first fraction to melt contains a higher proportion of alcohol than does the remaining solid block.

Partial crystallization is just the opposite. As a molten rock slowly cools, compounds with higher melting points crystallize first and the residual melt keeps changing in composition. This is analogous to slowly freezing the hard cider and thereby concentrating the alcohol in the residual unfrozen liquid.

Silica is concentrated in the low-melting-point fractions, especially when water is present. Therefore, both partial melting with small quantities of water present and partial crystallization during the ascent of magma to the surface can increase the silica content of the resulting volcanic rocks.

Magma appears to ascend a much greater distance in subduction volcanoes than in rift volcanoes. Also, the magma

supplying subduction volcanoes often must rise through ancient continental rocks, already high in silica, which greatly
increases their chance of contamination.

These concepts of partial melting, partial freezing, and
contamination all provide general explanations of the origin
of the many diverse volcanic rocks. Several specific explanations have also been proposed, and the arguments favoring
one process over another wax and wane on subtle details. The
problem is not a lack of explanation, but too many explanations. In fact, more than one process of variation is probably
at work. Truth is often a mixture of conflicting opinions.

The greater proportion of water and carbon dioxide dissolved in the magma of subduction volcanoes, coupled with
slightly lower eruption temperatures than in rift volcanoes,
leads to more explosive eruptions. The gas wants out, and the
less hot and therefore more viscous lava retards its escape,
resulting in explosive eruptions of volcanic ash. Subduction
eruptions often begin with explosive showers of ash, cinders,
and blocks and terminate with thick, viscous lava flows. Such
alternations of volcanic ash and lava flows build beautiful
steep cones like Mount Fuji, the archetype of classic volcanic
form (Figure 43).

About 40 subduction volcanoes erupt each year. A few,
like Stromboli in the Mediterranean, have been in nearly
continuous eruption for centuries. Others have erupted only
once in historic time. In general, the longer the period between eruptions, the greater the likelihood that an eruption
will be a major one. The products of subduction volcanoes
are largely explosive: ash, pumice, cinders, blocks, and molten lava bombs. This is in sharp contrast to the rift volcanoes
along the ocean ridges, whose products are mainly effusive
(nonexplosive) lava flows. The more notorious of the world's
volcanoes belong to the subduction clan: Vesuvius, Krakatau,
Mont Pelée, Katmai, Bezymianny, Mount St. Helens, and
Nevado del Ruiz.

Vesuvius buried Pompeii in A.D. 79 and provided a time
capsule of Roman art, architecture, and artifacts for its nine-
teenth- and twentieth-century excavators (Figure 44). Vesuvius was considered extinct before its violent eruption in

43 Mount Fuji, or Fuji-san, the archetypal volcano. The classic shape of this nearly perfect cone with graceful concave slopes, and its location near Tokyo, make it the world's best-known volcano. It rises to 3776 meters from a 30-kilometer-diameter base almost at sea level. Fuji-san embodies the beauty, majesty, and power of all nature. (Woodblock print by Hokusai [1760–1849] from his famous series, Thirty-Six Views of Mount Fuji.)

Roman times. It has had many eruptions since then, the latest in 1944.

In 1883 Krakatau, an island west of Java, disgorged 18 cubic kilometers of pumice and ash, producing huge sea waves called tsunamis more than 30 meters high that killed 36,000 people. The eruption formed a circular submarine depression called a caldera, 6 kilometers in diameter, in less than a day (Figures 45, 46, and 47).

The explosion of Krakatau produced worldwide effects. The noise was heard for thousands of kilometers, and the shock wave recorded on barographs around the world. The dust that was lifted into the stratosphere circled the globe,

44 Pompeii was buried beneath 6 meters of volcanic ash for nearly 2 thousand years. Its destroyer and preserver, Mount Vesuvius, is in the background. Airfall ash and nuées ardentes buried the town in one day in A.D. 79. Pliny, a Roman historian, described the eruption cloud as looking like a pine tree; a puzzling comparison until you note the tree behind the ruins.

producing astonishing visual effects: colorful sunrises and sunsets and a blue-green appearance of the sun and moon. The dust spread westward, encircling the equator in 2 weeks, then drifted both north and south. Average solar radiation in Europe decreased 10 percent over the next 3 years, and average world temperatures were below normal.

Mont Pelée in the West Indies annihilated the 28,000 inhabitants of the port of Saint Pierre on May 8, 1902. A glowing avalanche, or nuée ardente, rushed down the mountainside and the hot gases and ash bowled over and burned

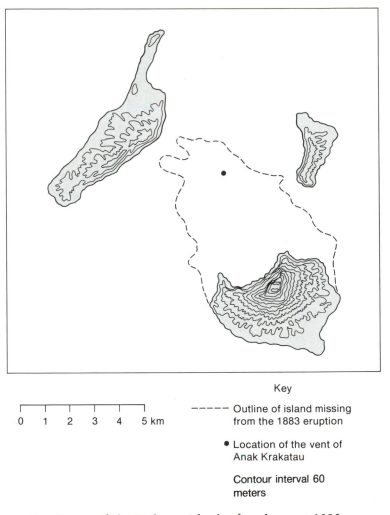

Key

0   1   2   3   4   5 km

----- Outline of island missing
from the 1883 eruption

● Location of the vent of
Anak Krakatau

Contour interval 60
meters

45 Sketch map of the Krakatau Islands after the great 1883 eruption. The missing area is 23 square kilometers; where a volcanic peak 450 meters high once stood, the water is now 275 meters deep. Anak Krakatau — child of Krakatau — began erupting in 1927. An island appeared in 1930 and has grown by small explosive eruptions and lava flows to a height of 200 meters and a diameter of nearly 2 kilometers.

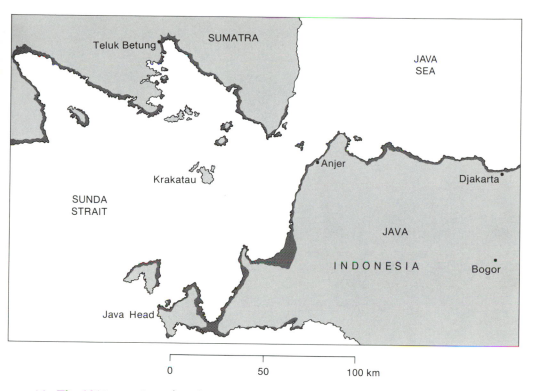

46 The 1883 eruption of Krakatau generated giant sea waves that killed 36,000 people. The shaded areas on the coasts of Java and Sumatra were the zones inundated by tsunamis from the great explosive eruptions and caldera collapse. (After C. J. Symons, ed., *The Eruption of Krakatoa.* Royal Society Report of the Krakatoa Committee, 1888.)

everything in their path, including ships in the harbor. The disaster took only a few minutes and left just two survivors in Saint Pierre (Figure 48).

Katmai on the Alaska Peninsula erupted for 2 days in June 1912. The ashfall totaled 20 cubic kilometers and practically buried Kodiak Island. A caldera 5 kilometers wide engulfed Katmai Peak, and 10 cubic kilometers of glowing avalanche deposits filled a valley 20 kilometers long and 3 kilometers wide to form the Valley of Ten Thousand Smokes.

Bezymianny on the Kamchatka Peninsula of Siberia erupted for the first time in recorded history on October 22,

47 Moderate explosive eruption of Anak Krakatau in January 1960, forming a 1000-meter-high ash cloud. The energy released in this explosion was less than one-millionth of the energy of the 1883 eruption.

48 Large nuée ardente eruption from Mont Pelée, several months after a similar cloud of hot gases and volcanic ash destroyed Saint Pierre and killed 28,000 people within minutes. (Photograph by A. Lacroix in 1902, courtesy of the American Museum of Natural History.)

49 Giant explosion cloud from Bezymianny Volcano, Kamchatka, March 30, 1956. The lower edge of the huge fan-shaped ash cloud is about 7 kilometers high and the top is about 35 kilometers high. (Photograph by I. V. Erov from 45 kilometers west of the volcano.)

1955, and culminated in a giant explosive eruption on March 30, 1956. The main eruption cloud reached 35 kilometers in height; large rocks were hurled 25 kilometers; a caldera 2 kilometers wide was formed; and nuées ardentes created a 3-cubic-kilometer deposit that Russian geologists call the Valley of Ten Thousand Smokes of Kamchatka (Figure 49). Fortunately at both Katmai and Bezymianny the area was almost uninhabited and no one was killed. Such eruptions in Japan, or Central America, or anywhere on the Ring of Fire where populations are dense would have been catastrophic.

A volcanic eruption doesn't have to be large to cause a catastrophe. The 1985 eruption of Nevado del Ruiz, a 5389-meter-high volcano in the Andes Range in Colombia, is a case in point. Although Ruiz is only 5 degrees north of the equator, its high summit is covered with a large snow and ice field (Figure 50). A relatively small eruption of hot pumice and ash

50 The summit of Colombia's Nevado del Ruiz Volcano, 5389 meters high, is covered by a 17-square-kilometer ice cap. A small pyroclastic eruption on November 13, 1985, melted about 5 to 10 percent of the ice cover and caused mudflows in the valleys draining the mountain's steep flanks. (Photograph by Robert Tilling, U.S. Geological Survey.)

jetted from the crater on November 13, landing on the icecap and causing sudden melting. A surge of meltwater sent massive mudflows down the steep canyons on the volcano's flanks. Fifty kilometers away and 5 kilometers below the summit of Ruiz the mudflow in the Lagunillas River inundated and destroyed the town of Armero (Figure 51). There and along other streams that drain Ruiz, mudflows killed 25,000 people.

Extremely large eruptions in prehistoric times have deposited enormous pyroclastic flows of pumice and ash that cover

51 The town of Armero, Colombia, 50 kilometers east and 5 kilometers below the summit of Ruiz Volcano, was destroyed by a massive mudflow that swept down the Lagunillas River from the November 13, 1985, eruption. About 22,000 people in Armero were killed by the sudden torrents of muddy water 3 to 5 meters deep.

thousands of square kilometers at several localities around the Ring of Fire. Volumes of magma more than 100 times greater than that hurled from Krakatau have been spewed forth in single eruptions. The message of such gigantic eruptions isn't imminent doom; they don't occur that often. To us their message is attention and respect; since the millions of people who reside on the Ring of Fire must live with these volcanic eruptions, it makes sense to try to understand them better.

6
Kilauea, Hawaii

52 Kilauea Iki, 1959. (Photograph by J. P. Eaton, U.S. Geological Survey.)

The marriage of Pele, goddess of earth and fire,
and Kamapuaa, god of water, was short and violent.
In a rage she routed him from her crater of fire
and chased him with streams of lava into the sea.

—HAWAIIAN LEGEND

. . . .

Kilauea Volcano on the Island of Hawaii, known also as the Big Island, is the most thoroughly studied volcano in the world (Figures 53 and 54). It is also one of the most active, with many eruptions and glowing lava lakes that stir and boil for years at a time (Color Plate 22). Almost all its eruptions are relatively quiet outpourings of fluid lavas. The word *quiet* can be misleading, though, for the vents often spurt fire fountains of incandescent lava several hundred meters high (Figure 52), which fall into lava ponds or feed lava flows. These outpourings of lava are quiet only in contrast to explosive volcanic eruptions, which produce fragmental debris and look more like huge detonations of dynamite.

Effusive eruptions of the Hawaiian type are comparatively safe to study at close range, and the Hawaiian Volcano Observatory has been at it since 1912. We were fortunate to be studying volcanoes in Hawaii during the early 1980s when major eruptions of both Kilauea and Mauna Loa volcanoes took place.

New Year of 1983 saw the start of the longest and largest rift eruption of Kilauea since written records began in 1823. By this writing (1989) the eruption, which shows no sign of stopping soon, has poured forth 850 million cubic meters of lava—enough to pave a highway circling the Earth four times. Flows have traveled 11 kilometers to the sea, covering

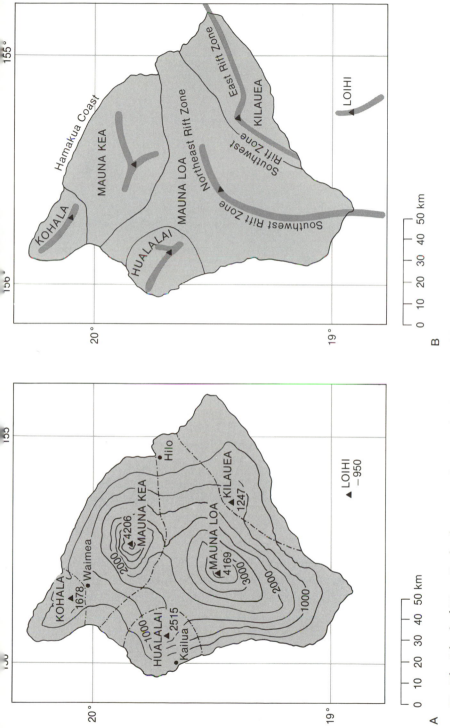

53 The Island of Hawaii, also known as the Big Island, is built of five volcanoes. Elevations in Map A are in meters. Rift zones shown in gray on Map B are zones of weakness from which numerous flank eruptions have occurred. Kilauea is erupting at the time of this writing (1989); Mauna Loa last erupted in 1984, and Hualalai in 1801. Mauna Kea's latest eruptions were about 4000 years ago, and Kohala's about 60,000 years ago. Loihi is a submarine volcano. It is presumed to be active because it has recurring earthquake swarms and because hot springs and young lava have been observed on Loihi from submersibles. (After D. W. Peterson and R. B. Moore, U.S. Geological Survey Professional Paper 1350, 1987, p. 151.)

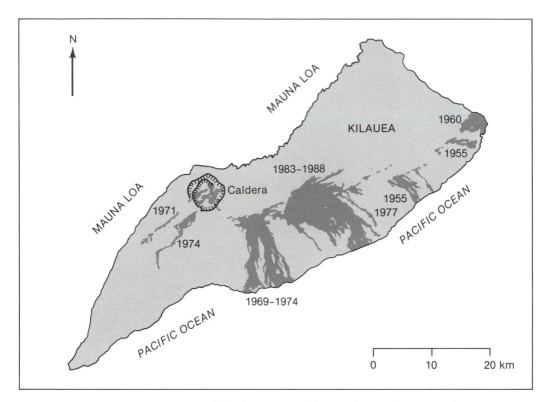

54 Most of the lava erupted from Kilauea since 1955 has come
from the East Rift Zone. Two eruptions (1971 and 1974) have
occurred on the Southwest Rift Zone, and 12 in the summit caldera
area. The flows labeled 1983–1988 are from the Puu Oo eruption.
(After Robin Holcomb and Christina Heliker, U.S. Geological Survey.)

60 square kilometers of land and adding 400,000 square
meters to the island. No lives have been lost, but at least 64
homes have been destroyed, and damage estimates exceed
$10 million.

January 1, 1983, was calm, but that was soon to change.
Not long after midnight the tremor alarm triggered phone
calls to staff members of the Volcano Observatory. Hurrying
to the observatory, perched on the rim of Kilauea's 3-by-5-
kilometer-wide caldera, we soon learned that all three signs
of an impending eruption were taking place.

Volcanic tremor, a continuous low-frequency vibration of the ground, was being recorded on seismographs near the East Rift Zone of Kilauea. Tremor occurs when magma is moving rapidly in underground conduits. Seismographs also showed earthquake swarms at shallow depths beneath the east rift, indicating that new fractures were forming. Tilt-meters showed that the summit area was subsiding. A tilt-meter works like an extremely sensitive carpenter's level, and can detect changes in slope of 1 part per million— equivalent to a 1-millimeter rise of one end of a line that is 1 kilometer long.

Tremor, earthquake swarms, and summit deflation all in-dicated that magma from a storage zone beneath Kilauea Caldera was being injected into the east rift (Figures 55 and 56). These shallow intrusions into the weak rift zones on the flank of the volcano are not uncommon; they may happen several times a year. Some reach the surface and erupt, others do not. The same question was on everyone's mind: Would this be another aborted alarm, or would this shallow intru-sion become an eruption?

All day on January 2 the tremor, earthquakes, and subsi-dence continued. The earthquakes were clustered on the middle east rift, about 10 to 20 kilometers east of Kilauea's summit. Finally, past midnight on January 3, fountains broke out in Napau Crater, which lies 15 kilometers from the sum-mit on the East Rift Zone. By morning, fissures in a broken line 6 kilometers long were erupting "curtains of fire" in a remote, inaccessible forest. During the next 12 days various vents along this fissure system erupted intermittently, but only geologists and TV crews in helicopters were able to see the spectacular start of this long-lasting eruption.

There had been a lengthy prelude to this lava outbreak, and many clues had come from careful observations of small earthquakes and deformations of the ground surface. Ki-lauea's magma rises from a depth of 60 kilometers or more and accumulates temporarily in a reservoir a few kilometers beneath the summit. As the underground reservoir inflates, magma pressure increases until the rocks above or to the sides of the reservoir crack and fail. Molten rock then pushes

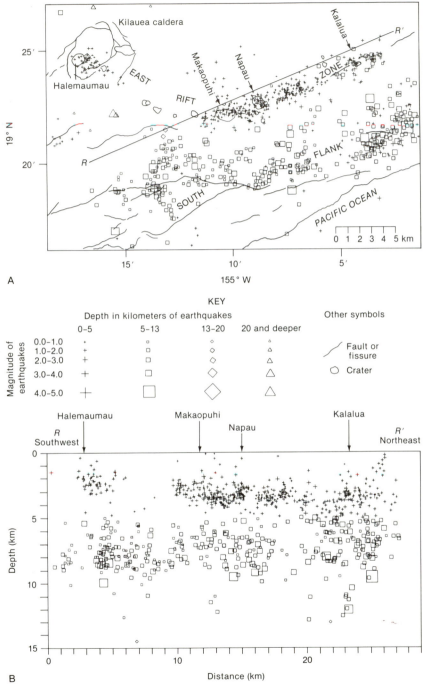

A

Kilauea caldera

Halemaumau

EAST

RIFT

Makaopuhi

Napau

ZONE

Kalalua

R'

FLANK

SOUTH

PACIFIC OCEAN

0 1 2 3 4 5 km

25'

19° N

20'

R

15'   10'   5'

155° W

KEY

Depth in kilometers of earthquakes   Other symbols

Magnitude of earthquakes

	0–5	5–13	13–20	20 and deeper
0.0–1.0				
1.0–2.0				
2.0–3.0				
3.0–4.0				
4.0–5.0				

⟋ Fault or fissure

⬡ Crater

Halemaumau   Makaopuhi

Napau

Kalalua

R
Southwest

R'
Northeast

Depth (km)

0

5

10

15

0   10   20

Distance (km)

B

into these fractures, erupting at the surface (Color Plate 20) or halting underground as a shallow intrusion into the rift zones on the volcano's flanks. There are two persistent zones of weakness in the sides of Kilauea: the East Rift Zone and the Southwest Rift Zone.

As an injection of molten rock moves out into one of the rift zones, earthquake swarms outline the moving magma's progress. As the reservoir deflates, the summit subsides. Magma moving rapidly underground also causes volcanic tremor. By studying seismographs from many locations on the volcano and by measuring small changes in uplift, subsidence, expansion, or contraction of the volcano's surface, these underground movements of magma at Kilauea are routinely detected and mapped.

Twelve intrusions of magma occurred beneath the east rift from 1978 through 1982; only two of these erupted to the surface, one in 1979 and a very small event in 1980. Besides these rapid intrusions into new underground cracks, slower leakage from the summit reservoir into existing fractures caused additional swelling of the east rift in the area where the 1983 eruption fissures opened. This region was ready for a major eruption.

The fissures erupted intermittently between January 3 and 23; then lava emission stopped and the summit of Kilauea began to reinflate. Almost 5 square kilometers of land had been covered with 14 million cubic meters of basaltic lava flows. Since short-lived volcanic events are common in Hawaii many people thought the eruption was over, but on

55   *A.* Locations of earthquakes during January 1983, beneath the summit and the East Rift Zone of Kilauea. The shallow quakes between Makaopuhi and Kalalua were caused by the magma forcing its way into fractures at the start of the Puu Oo eruption. *B.* Earthquake locations projected into the cross section show that the magma conduit had its axis at about 3 kilometers depth. (From E. W. Wolfe and others, U.S. Geological Survey Professional Paper 1350, 1987, pp. 482–483.)

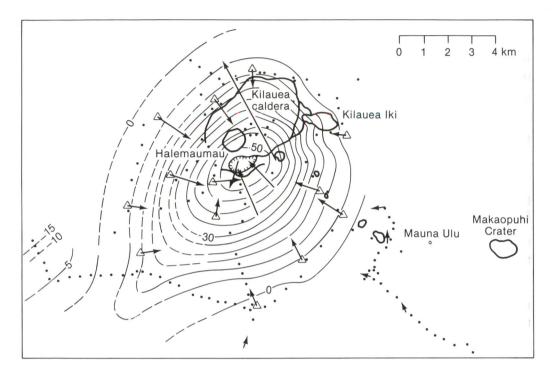

KEY

• Leveling bench mark

Spirit-level tilt station with direction and amount of tilt change

⌐ Crater or caldera rim

Contour of elevation change—Dashed where approximately located; hachures indicate closed low. Contour interval 5 centimeters

56 Subsidence of the summit of Kilauea took place as magma drained into the east rift to supply the start of the Puu Oo eruption. The level surveys that determined this change were made during September 27 to October 5, 1982, and repeated on February 7 to 11, 1983. A continuously recording tiltmeter on the northwest side of Kilauea Caldera showed that nearly all this subsidence occurred on January 2–7, 1983. (From E. W. Wolfe and others, U.S. Geological Survey Professional Paper 1350, 1987, p. 488.)

February 10 minor lava emission resumed, and from February 25 to March 4 vigorous lava fountains spewed from a vent about two-thirds of the way down the original fissure system. Again the eruption stopped and tiltmeters at the summit, which had indicated subsidence, reversed direction and showed reinflation.

When summit inflation recovered to a critical level, would the eruption resume again? The answer was yes. During the third episode lava gushed forth from March 28 to April 9, and in episode 4, at a new site uprift near the center of the original fissure system, lava fountains erupted from June 13 to 17. Between July 1983 and July 1986 the general eruption pattern — short periods of high lava fountains from the same vent area lasting a few hours to days, separated by longer repose periods averaging about 1 month — was repeated an astounding 43 more times.

Although this 3-year period of activity began to seem repetitious, geologists in charge of field observations discovered interesting trends and changes in eruptive habits that throw light on the inner workings of Kilauea Volcano. Figure 57 shows the cumulative volume of lava produced by the first 20 eruptive episodes, and the subsidence-inflation cycles of the summit magma chamber. Notice how much steeper the inward tilt of the summit is during an eruption episode than is the outward tilt during reinflation. This indicates that the rate at which lava was erupted was much faster than the rate of supply of magma from depth.

The average rate of lava emission during the eruption has been 160 million cubic meters per year (Figure 58). As the magma erupts most of the volcanic gases boil out in the vigorous fountains. However, some gas stays trapped in bubble holes, called vesicles, in the solidifying lava. To calculate the magma volume, the volume of the vesicles — about 25 percent — has to be subtracted. Thus the average rate of magma erupted has been 120 million cubic meters per year, close to the long-term magma supply rate at Kilauea. This balance is confirmed by the tilt record during the eruption.

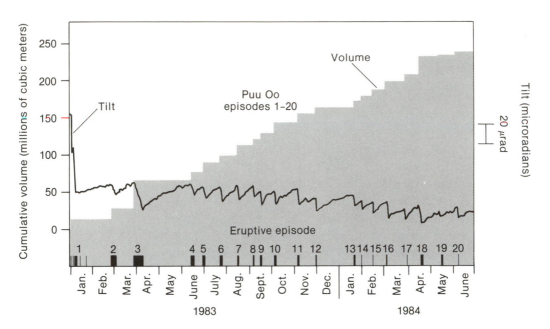

57 From 1983 until 1986 Puu Oo erupted in intermittent episodes. During repose periods the summit tilt showed slow uplift, and during episodes of vigorous lava fountaining (shown in black with episode number) the tilt indicated rapid subsidence of Kilauea's summit area. The substantial tilt loss at the beginning of the eruption (episode 1) was caused by the large volume of magma needed to fill the fracture system that initiated the eruption. (From E. W. Wolfe and others, U.S. Geological Survey Professional Paper 1350, 1987, pp. 490–91.)

Although the summit rose and fell with the eruptive episodes, the net tilt change since episode 1 has been small. Such balance between eruption rate and resupply of magma implies the eruption could be very long-lasting.

As the eruption progressed the eruptive episodes became shorter and the rate of lava emission more rapid (Figure 59), maintaining roughly the same lava production per episode (about 13 million cubic meters). As the discharge rates increased the lava fountains grew higher, exceeding 400 meters during episodes 24 to 30. This increase in vigor may have

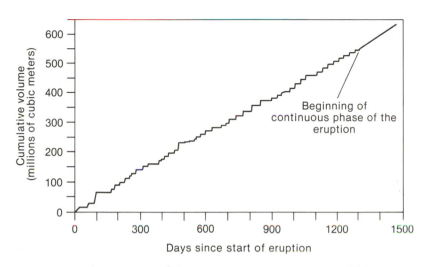

58 Lava production rate of the Puu Oo eruption, January 1983 to December 1986. Lava production rate during the Puu Oo eruption to this time (1983–1989) has been remarkably steady. In the episodic phase of the eruption, each fountaining event produced about 13 million cubic meters of lava. Repose periods between episodes lasted about a month. Since the continuous phase began in July 1986, the slow but steady lava emission has amounted to about 0.4 to 0.5 million cubic meters per day. (From G. E. Ulrich, U.S. Geological Survey.)

been caused in part by improved plumbing. Magma coursing underground during each episode of eruption probably enlarged the conduits. Magma is hot enough (about 1150°C) to melt the wall rocks, enlarging the channels through which it moves. This is also thought to be the reason that a fissure eruption usually becomes localized at a single vent as a Hawaiian eruption progresses; where a fissure is narrow, less lava flows through, and the crack tends to heal shut as lava cools and clings to the wall rock. Wider places in the fissure are enlarged as hot magma rapidly surges through them, and the widest spot usually captures most of the flow.

Lava temperatures near the vents increased as the eruption progressed from about 1120° (episode 1) to 1140°C (episode

18), and the magnesium content of the basalt increased from about 6 percent to 7.5 percent. These changes are interpreted to mean that some of the magma which was erupted in the early episodes had been stored in the rift zone before eruption, cooling and precipitating olivine, a mineral rich in magnesium, and other silicate minerals. Later in the eruption,

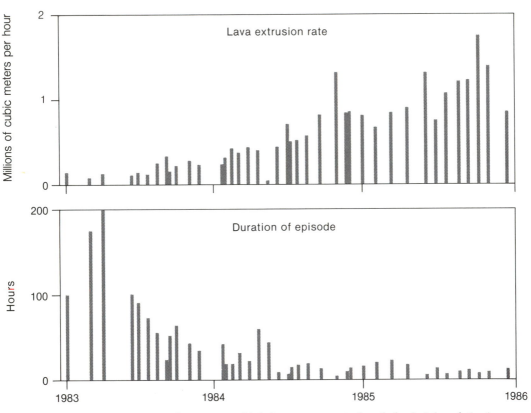

59 The rate at which lava was erupted and the height of the lava fountains generally increased as the Puu Oo eruption progressed. However, the duration of each episode generally decreased. The net effect was to maintain a roughly equal amount of lava (about 13 million cubic meters) erupted in each episode. (From G. E. Ulrich, U.S. Geological Survey.)

The development of Kilauea Volcano's Puu Oo eruption, 1983 to 1988

Plate 1 High lava fountains and rivers of molten rock gushed out repeatedly during the episodic phase of the eruption. (Photograph by J. D. Griggs, U.S. Geological Survey, January 31, 1984.)

Plate 2 A 30-meter-high "curtain of fire" spurts from a long fracture at the beginning of the eruption. (Photograph by J. D. Griggs, U.S. Geological Survey.)

Plate 3 Early in the eruption, a large lava flow spreads through the forest from the fissure in the background. (Photograph by J. D. Griggs, U.S. Geological Survey.)

Plate 4 An arching lava fountain, 10 to 15 meters high, is hurled from an early vent. (Photograph by J. D. Griggs, U.S. Geological Survey.)

Plate 5 Geologist measures the temperature of an aa flow. (Photograph by George Ulrich, U.S. Geological Survey.)

Plate 6 Four-hundred-meter-high lava fountain during episode 31 of the eruption dwarfs a Civil Defense helicopter. (Photograph by J. D. Griggs, U.S. Geological Survey.)

Plate 7 Fume cloud from a vigorous eruptive episode as seen from the Hawaiian Volcano Observatory 20 kilometers away. (Photograph by J. D. Griggs, U.S. Geological Survey.)

Plate 8 Thin strands of volcanic glass spun out in a lava fountain are called Pele's hair. Individual strands often reach 20 centimeters in length. (Photograph by D. W. Peterson, U.S. Geological Survey.)

Plate 9 River of molten lava 10 to 20 meters wide flows from Puu Oo and forms the central channel of a black aa lava flow. The trees on the left side of the flow are about 15 meters tall. (Photograph by J. D. Griggs, U.S. Geological Survey.)

Plate 10 The advancing front of a 2- to 3-meter-thick lava flow moves slowly, but stops for no one. (Photograph by J. D. Griggs, U.S. Geological Survey.)

Plate 11 Molten rock wells up in a 100-meter-wide lava lake and spills down a deep channel (left center) to feed crusted-over lava tubes. Pahoehoe flows from this continuous phase of the eruption moved slowly but inexorably down the southeast flank of Kilauea toward the sea in the background. (Photograph by J. D. Griggs, U.S. Geological Survey.)

Plate 12 A pahoehoe lava flow creeps across a lawn before destroying another home on its way to the sea. (Photograph by J. D. Griggs, U.S. Geological Survey.)

Plate 13 As lava pours into the sea, glow from the stream of red-hot rock illuminates the steam cloud. (Photograph by Jane Takahashi, U.S. Geological Survey.)

most of the erupted lava was from hotter, more primitive magma in the summit reservoir.

With the vent localized in one spot along the fissure (episodes 4–47), the eruption began to build a major cinder and spatter cone around it (Figure 60). The cone was 20 meters high after episode 4, 130 meters high following episode 20, and by 1986 had reached a height of 255 meters with a base about 1 kilometer in diameter. This imposing cone became a landmark visible from roads 30 kilometers away, and was given the Hawaiian name Puu Oo, "Hill of the Oo Bird." The entire eruption from its onset in 1983 is known as the Puu Oo eruption of Kilauea Volcano.

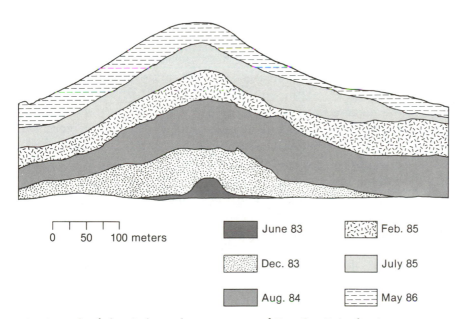

0 50 100 meters	

■ June 83   ▨ Feb. 85

□ Dec. 83   ▨ July 85

▨ Aug. 84   ≡ May 86

60 Growth of the cinder and spatter cone of Puu Oo. Episodes 4 to 47 (1983–1986) were erupted from this vent and built the cone to a height of 255 meters with a base about 1 kilometer wide. These profiles are looking up the rift zone, and are not vertically exaggerated. Since 1986 growth has stopped and slumping has begun to modify the cone's shape. (From Christina Heliker, U.S. Geological Survey.)

The lava falling back from the high fountains formed aa flows that moved away from the vent to the northeast, east, or southeast for 5 to 8 kilometers. Flows of this type are generally about ¼ to ½ kilometer wide and 3 to 5 meters thick, fed by a central river of incandescent lava about 10 to 20 meters across. The central stream moves quite rapidly — 10 to 20 kilometers per hour — but as it spreads beneath the dark rubbly blocks near the front of the flow, it slows dramatically. The overall advance rates of the Puu Oo aa flows were only a few hundred meters per hour. Although people had plenty of time to evacuate, several homes were crushed and burned as the relentless aa flows covered parts of a rural subdivision 7 kilometers southeast of the vent.

The reason the early eruptions at Puu Oo were episodic and geyserlike is not clear. Two factors seem to have been involved; first, some sort of off-on valve in the conduit between the summit magma reservoir and the vent, which was sensitive to pressure changes. As the summit inflated and the magma pressure increased, new magma would push through the conduit; as the summit deflated and pressure dropped, the magma flow would stop. The second factor was the gas content in the magma. Lava would appear in the vent for several days before the fountaining started, and slow overflow of the vent would precede the high fountaining. Apparently a gas-poor, dense plug of lava had to overflow before the strong boiling of gas that propelled the lava fountains began. As fountaining removed the top of the magma column, pressure was reduced on magma below and it too would flash into boiling effervescence. This discharge continued at a high rate until the available magma and gas were exhausted.

The gases dissolved in magma are mainly water, carbon dioxide, and sulfur dioxide. At Kilauea they amount to only about 1 percent of the magma by weight. However, at high temperatures and low surface pressures, these gases vigorously boil out of the magma, and the gas volume can be many times the molten lava volume.

The high lava fountains produced large amounts of pumice and Pele's hair. Pumice is a quickly cooled volcanic rock that traps the volcanic gases in tiny bubble holes; in a sense it is a solidified lava foam. The ratio of gas bubble holes to glassy volcanic rock is so high that large pumice lumps are as light as Styrofoam and float easily on water. Fine strands of volcanic glass that spin off from molten drops of lava whirling in the turbulent lava fountains are called Pele's hair. Both pumice lumps and Pele's hair were often blown several kilometers downwind from the lava fountains. Heavier lumps of solidified lava called cinders or scoria and still-molten lumps of spatter accumulate near the base of fountains and build the cinder and spatter cone around the vent. The Puu Oo cone grew highest on the southwest rim of the vent because the prevailing northeast trade winds piled most of the fallout from the lava fountains on the downwind side.

Puu Oo's seventeenth eruptive episode brought an answer to a long-standing scientific question. For years volcanologists had speculated on what the underground connections of Kilauea and nearby Mauna Loa volcanoes might be, and whether the activity of one would affect the other. Mauna Loa began a major eruption on March 25, 1984, and by March 30 was pouring a large flow of lava toward the city of Hilo from a vent at 2900 meters elevation (Color Plates 18 and 19). Puu Oo was expected to erupt in late March, and everyone waited to see if Mauna Loa's eruption would affect the Kilauea activity or vice versa. Episode 17 arrived on schedule with 100-meter-high fountains that lasted 23 hours and poured out 10 million cubic meters of lava. It was rare and marvelous to see both volcanoes erupting at the same time.

Even though the vent at Puu Oo was more than 2000 meters below the Mauna Loa vent, neither eruption had any apparent effect on the other. Although both Kilauea and Mauna Loa volcanoes may get their magma from the same general deep source, it is clear that there is no hydraulic connection between the shallow magma reservoirs of the two volcanoes.

Three and a half years after the start of the Puu Oo eruption, episode 48 in July 1986 brought a significant change. Fractures opened both up- and downrift from Puu Oo; a new vent became established about 3 kilometers downrift and activity was now focused there. Smooth-surfaced lava flows called pahoehoe issued slowly and steadily from this new vent, building a broad, low pile of solidified lava around it and ponding the upwelling magma into a 100-meter-wide active lava lake. Lava sometimes overflowed the rim of the pond, but more often it escaped through a tunnel to feed pahoehoe flows that slowly advanced through lava tubes beneath their surfaces.

In contrast to the earlier episodic pulses, the eruption now has been nearly continuous, pouring out lava at a rate of almost ½ million cubic meters per day for more than 2 years. Although the pahoehoe lava flows from this phase of the eruption advance more slowly than the aa flows from the earlier intermittent eruptions, they have slowly but inexorably moved down the southeast flank of the rift to the sea. Flows reached the sea in November 1986, destroying rural homes and covering a highway on the way. More homes were destroyed in December. Lava has been intermittently pouring into the ocean since that time, adding new land to the island.

The molten rock moves in lava tubes beneath the surface of the flows from the lava lake to the sea, a distance of about 11 kilometers. Sometimes the tubes become blocked with chunks of lava crust. When this happens the lava lake rises and overflows, or new flows break out from the lava tubes above the blockage. Often the tubes clear themselves and flows to the sea are reestablished. Small explosions of steam and lava sometimes occur as the red-hot rock slips into the sea, but usually a pillar of steam is all that marks a remarkably docile meeting of fire and water (Figure 61).

As the molten lava is suddenly quenched by the sea, some of it shatters into sand-sized fragments. This new sand is swept along by shoreline currents and has formed large black sand beaches where once the surf pounded on bare rock ledges. These new beaches extend for several kilometers along the coast, well beyond the edges of the flows entering the sea.

The billowing surface of the pahoehoe flows that form most of the land that has been added to the island looks like easy walking, but its appearance is deceptive. Not only is it possible to break through the surface into a lava tube, but recently large sections of the newly added land have started to slump into the sea. This happens without warning and poses a major danger to volcano watchers who seek a close view of molten lava meeting the ocean.

Why did the eruption become slow and steady after the new vent opened downrift? Part of the explanation may be that much of the volcanic gases keep venting from the Puu Oo cone, and not enough remains in the magma that supplies the lava lake to drive high fountains.

The gases also seem to be responsible for another phenomenon, a haze of volcanic fume locally called vog (volcanic smog) that has plagued parts of the Big Island since the lava began entering the ocean in late 1986. The ingredients of this vog come not only from the gases from Puu Oo and the active lava lake, but apparently also from an aerosol of hydrochloric acid droplets formed in the steam plume where the lava meets the sea. The trade winds generally blow the vog out to sea near the eruption, but it usually eddies back on the west side of the island — much to the irritation of residents used to warm, clear breezes and unobscured sunset views.

Although the Puu Oo eruption is the largest rift eruption in recorded history, it is not unprecedented. Summit eruptions of Kilauea were nearly continuous from 1823 to 1924, and one prehistoric east rift eruption appears to have been much more voluminous than the present output. Each new eruption leads to important insights on how volcanoes work. As old questions are answered, new ones arise. How do the lava tubes form, block up, and reopen? Why does some of the new land added to Hawaii in this eruption slump into the sea in sections larger than a football field? How does the hydrochloric-acid vog form in the steam plumes where the lava enters the sea? There is much for the present group of scientists at the Hawaiian Volcano Observatory to learn. There always will be.

7
Hot Spots

61   Lava lake in Hawaii. (Photograph by D. H. Richter, U.S. Geological Survey.)

Stones rot. Only the chants remain.

—POLYNESIAN SAYING

. . . .

The close connection between the edges of the moving plates of the Earth's crust and volcanoes has been emphasized in earlier chapters. Why then is the Island of Hawaii, with two of the world's most active volcanoes, located right in the middle of the Pacific plate (Figure 62)? Only 5 percent of the world's active volcanoes are located within plates, but even so there must be some reason for their existence.

There are some obvious differences between the Hawaiian volcanoes, which form a linear belt or chain, and volcanoes located on plate margins. Topography is one. A profile section of the Hawaiian Islands chain is completely different from a cross section of a spreading ridge or a subduction zone (Figure 63).

Another major difference is the age distribution of Hawaiian volcanoes compared to that of plate margin volcanoes. Geologists have recognized for more than 100 years that the islands in the Hawaiian chain become older as you move from the southeast to the northwest. Since 1800, eruptions have occurred only on Hawaii, at the southeast end of the chain; the islands to the northwest are lower and more eroded. The chain extends to Midway Island, 2500 kilometers northwest of the Big Island of Hawaii, where only a coral atoll cap covering a submerged volcanic peak marks the largely submarine ridge. The ages of the volcanic rocks of the Hawaiian Islands, obtained by radioactivity dating, confirm this picture. Rocks on the Big Island are all less than 1 million

62 The Hawaiian Islands rise from the southeast end of a 6000-kilometer-long dogleg chain of seamounts. The portion north of the bend is called the Emperor Seamounts; that south of the bend is called the Hawaiian Ridge. (Map from *World Ocean Floor Panorama* by Bruce C. Heezen and Marie Tharp, initiated and supported by the Office of Naval Research. Copyright Marie Tharp, 1977. Reproduced by permission of Marie Tharp, all rights reserved.)

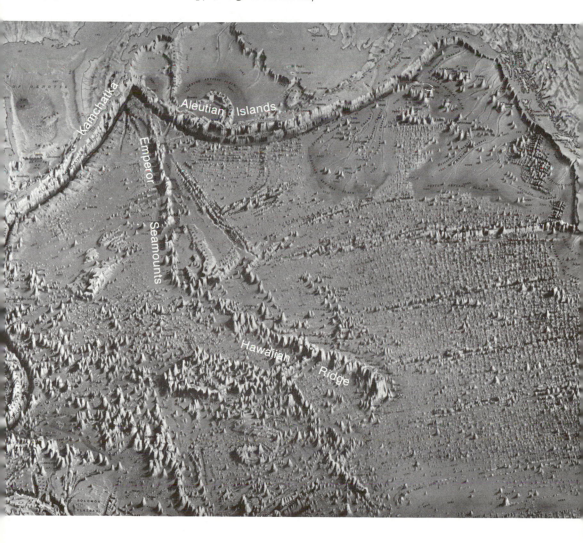

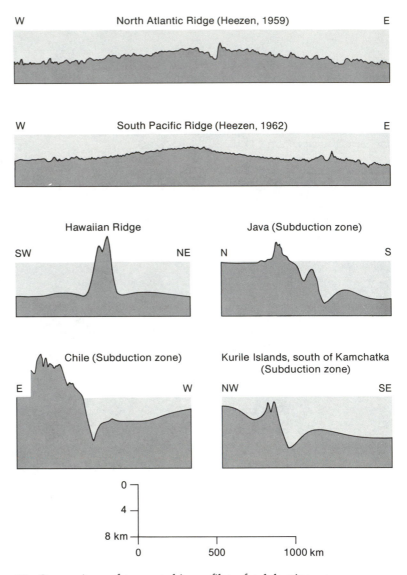

63 Comparison of topographic profiles of subduction zones, mid-ocean ridges, and Hawaii. Vertical scale is exaggerated 40 times. Island arcs and compressional mountains are basically asymmetrical, whereas mid-ocean ridges and Hawaii are symmetrical about a central axis. The width of the mid-ocean ridges is caused by seafloor spreading.

years old; most of the rocks on Oahu, the location of Honolulu and Pearl Harbor, are 2 to 3 million years old; and the
ancient lava flows on Kauai, northwest of Oahu, are about 5
million years old (Figure 64).

This pattern of age distribution of Hawaiian volcanic rock
is strikingly different from that of plate margin volcanoes. In
subduction zones and on the oceanic ridges, the young volcanoes form a line along the seam of the plates; and on the
oceanic ridges there is a progressive aging of the volcanic
rocks on either side of the active belt. The Hawaiian chain is
just the opposite: the volcanoes get older along the crest of
the chain, instead of across the crest of the volcanic belt.

Earthquakes, those close companions of active volcanoes,
also show an unusual pattern in Hawaii. Earthquakes occur

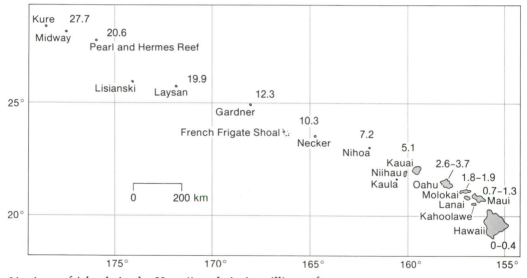

64 Ages of islands in the Hawaiian chain in millions of years.
Islands get progressively older to the northwest. The apparent rate of
movement away from the Hawaiian hot spot (deep source of magma)
is about 9 to 10 centimeters per year. (Data from D. A. Clague and
G. B. Dalrymple, U.S. Geological Survey, Professional Paper 1350,
1987, p. 16.)

along the entire length of subduction zones and oceanic ridges, but in Hawaii they are common only at the southeast end of the chain, mostly beneath the Big Island.

The data from more than 30,000 microearthquakes occurring near Kilauea Volcano on Hawaii, and the pattern of tilting that indicates swelling and contraction of a shallow reservoir of molten rock (a magma chamber), suggest an interesting subsurface model of a Hawaiian volcano (Figure 65).

Charting the location of the earthquakes at depth outlines the conduits through which the molten rock forces its way upward. The propelling force is the buoyancy of the lighter

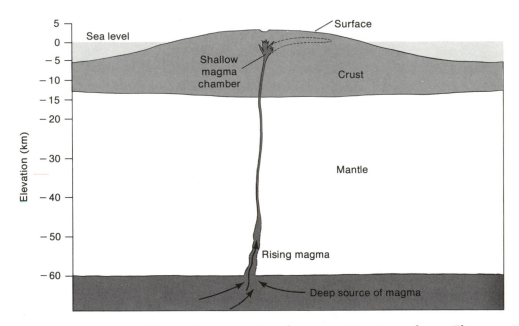

65 Schematic cross section of an active Hawaiian volcano. The vertical scale is exaggerated two times. The dotted line extending to the right from the shallow magma chamber is an inferred zone of feeder dikes to a rift zone. The deep source of magma, below 50 to 60 kilometers, and the shallow storage zone at 3 to 6 kilometers beneath the surface, are the vital parts of the active system. (After Jerry Eaton, U.S. Geological Survey.)

molten rock surrounded by more dense crystalline rocks. As the magma rises, the hard surrounding rocks are cracked open by changing pressures and temperatures, causing earthquakes.

The deep source of magma appears to be within the plastic layer 50 to 60 kilometers beneath the Pacific plate,the maximum depth of the earthquakes. Graphs of the locations of the intermediate-to-deep earthquakes, 10 to 60 kilometers beneath Kilauea, over a period of years outline a zone shaped like an inverted funnel 5 to 50 kilometers in diameter and 50 kilometers high, which allows the deep magma to come up into a shallow magma chamber 3 to 6 kilometers beneath the summit. This shallow chamber is bounded by a region of many microearthquakes, but has almost no earthquakes inside of it. Most earthquakes are thought to originate from the cracking and slipping of brittle rocks that suddenly fail by fracture. Plastic or liquid rock in a magma chamber can deform without breaking and thus doesn't cause earthquakes (Figure 66).

The tilt pattern near the summit of Kilauea supports this magma chamber model. Just as the pattern of tilting on the surface of an inflating balloon would indicate the radius of the balloon, the pattern of tilt at Kilauea indicates a pressure center about 4 kilometers deep. In this balloon analogy, the deep source of magma is the pump, the inverted-funnel conduit is the connecting hose, and the shallow magma chamber is the balloon.

The pattern of slow outward tilting or inflation of Kilauea prior to an eruption and rapid inward tilting or deflation during a flank eruption indicates a slow, almost continuous movement of magma from the deep source to the shallow chamber, and rapid and intermittent eruptions from the shallow chamber to the surface. Because the rate of movement of magma from depth to the shallow chamber generally does not keep pace with the surface eruption rate, the eruption eventually stops until the shallow chamber is recharged. The eruption at Puu Oo has been an exception. Since the steady-state lava emission began there in 1986, the lava has been

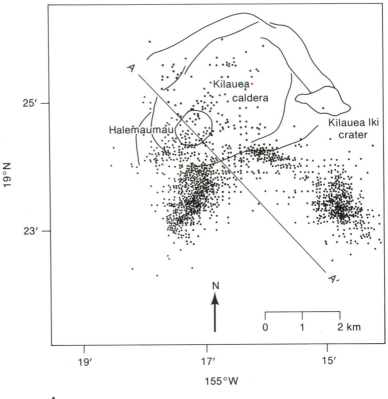

A

66 *A.* Map view of locations of shallow microearthquakes beneath Kilauea Volcano in Hawaii. Earthquakes are caused by rock fracture. Zones of no earthquakes are therefore regions of low stress or very low strength. Since high stresses prevail near most active volcanoes, the lack of earthquakes in a region surrounded by them suggests a plastic zone occupied by magma. The dense clusters of microearthquakes shown on the map indicate the beginning of the rift zones. *B. Opposite.* Cross section of Kilauea caldera to a depth of 12 kilometers. (Data from Robert Koyanagi, U.S. Geological Survey.)

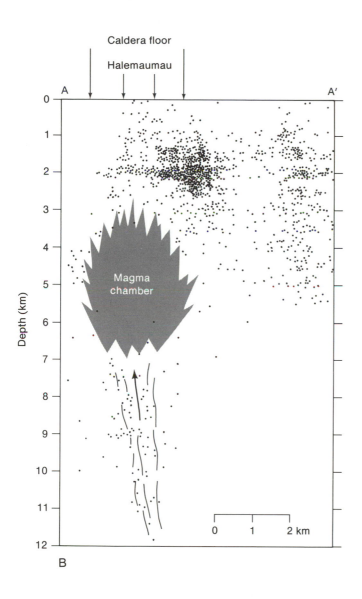

slowly but continuously resupplied from depth. The lack of significant inflation or deflation of the summit of Kilauea during this period supports this conclusion.

But how does this relate to the origin and continuing vigor of the Hawaiian volcanic chain? There must be something unique about the location of the Island of Hawaii. Somehow deep magma must be more available at this location. Tuzo

Wilson, a Canadian geophysicist, suggested an elegantly simple explanation that fits neatly with the movement of the Pacific plate. He envisioned a hot plume of magma originating deep beneath the plate. This plume, or hot spot, stays in the same location for millions of years as the plate slides over this source of magma. A volcano grows over the hot spot and drifts away with the slowly moving plate to be replaced by a new volcano growing over the same hot spot, like smoke signals drifting in a gentle wind (Figure 67). Most geologists now accept the hot-spot idea, but the concept is still more controversial than the larger scheme of plate tectonics.

The problem, of course, is in explaining the character of the hot spot. What keeps generating new magma at a relatively fixed spot within the Earth? The best theory now seems to be that the heat source of the hot spot is in the deep mantle, beneath the plastic layer. This implies that hot-spot volcanoes may have even deeper ultimate sources for their magma than the volcanic belts along the plate margins (Figure 68).

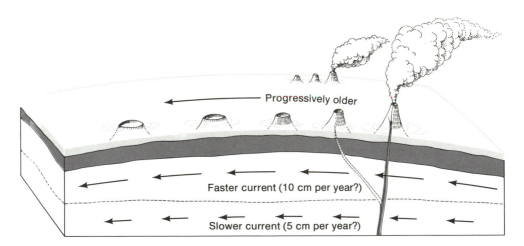

67   Original diagram used by Tuzo Wilson to suggest the origin of the Hawaiian Islands. The plate slowly moves over a relatively fixed source of magma, forming a new volcano as the older volcanoes are carried downstream. (From J. Tuzo Wilson, "Continental Drift." Copyright © 1963 by Scientific American, Inc. All rights reserved.)

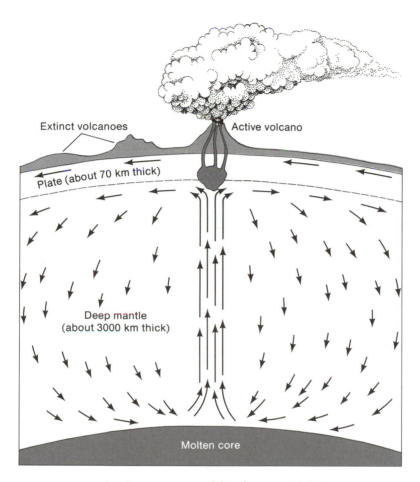

68 Deep mantle plumes generated by slow convection currents are one explanation of the relatively fixed position of hot-spot volcanic sources. This concept, originated by Jason Morgan, is illustrated here. (After G. B. Dalrymple, E. A. Silver, and E. D. Jackson, "Origin of the Hawaiian Islands," *American Scientist* 61, March 1973, p. 306.)

If the hot-spot theory is correct, the aging of volcanoes away from the hot spot should match the rate of plate movement. The magnetic stripe pattern on the ocean floor indicates the Pacific plate is moving northwest at about 10 centimeters per year. If Kauai has drifted northwest during the 5 to 6 million years since its lavas erupted, it should be 500 to

600 kilometers away from where it formed, which is the present location of the Big Island. The actual distance is 560 kilometers, a striking verification of Wilson's idea or an amazing coincidence, depending on your belief.

Beyond Midway Island, the Hawaiian chain is a submerged line of seamounts continuing northwest another 1000 kilometers. After that, it meets a submerged mountain chain, the Emperor Seamounts, which trend north-northwest another 2500 kilometers toward Kamchatka. The Emperor Seamounts are thought to be a dogleg of the Hawaiian chain formed when the drift of the Pacific plate was more northward than its present northwestward movement. The change in direction of plate movement, as estimated from the location of the bend, occurred about 43 million years ago.

The hot-spot explanation of the Hawaiian chain suggests that future islands will form to the southeast of the Big Island. Loihi seamount, 28 kilometers southeast of the Island of Hawaii, looks as if it will be that next island. Loihi is 970 meters below sea level, with two deep craters indenting its summit. Recent dives in the submersible *Alvin* have revealed pillow-lava flows on Loihi that appear to be very young. Warm springs with dissolved carbon dioxide have also been observed and sampled there.

Swarms of earthquakes were recorded beneath Loihi in 1971–1972 and 1975 and may have been related to submarine eruptions, though this correlation is not certain. Whether vigorously active or not, it will probably be thousands of years before Loihi becomes the next Hawaiian Island.

The great strength of the plate tectonics theory is that its predictions are substantiated by clues found in so many places around the world. The plates have left their tracks in the form of volcanic scars and magnetic fields, and those tracks yield a complex yet consistent global pattern.

At least two more seamount chains beneath the South Pacific indicate other major hot spots beneath the Pacific plate. Yellowstone Park, on the North America plate, has been suggested as an active continental hot spot with the

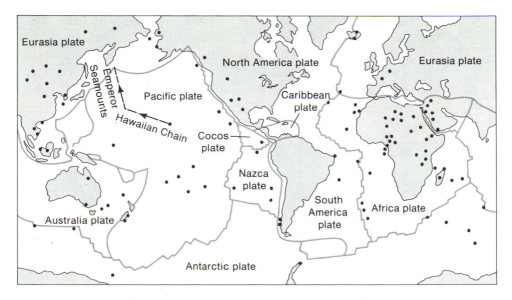

69 Present world hot spots and their relation to the major plates.
Hot-spot tracks, as illustrated by the Hawaii-Emperor trend, reveal
past plate motions. Some geologists prefer a smaller number of hot
spots. (After Kevin C. Burke and J. Tuzo Wilson, "Hot Spots on the
Earth's Surface." Copyright © 1976 by Scientific American, Inc. All
rights reserved.)

Snake River volcanic plain its earlier track. The Galapagos
Islands on the equator off the west coast of South America is
another group of very active volcanoes of probable hot-spot
origin (Figure 69).

The hot-spot idea even offers a solution to the Iceland
anomaly: the problem of why Iceland is the only major part
of the Mid-Atlantic Ridge out of water. If Iceland is a hot
spot that has become straddled by the ridge, then it has volcanoes of dual origin — both hot-spot and oceanic-ridge. This is
an attractive explanation of the extra volcanism that has built
Iceland above the sea.

No islands of similar origin could be more unlike than
Hawaii and Iceland. Iceland is a rugged, nearly treeless land

of harsh climate, inhabited by strong Vikings who have stal-wartly maintained their culture and independence. Hawaii is a tropical garden, soft and seductive, inhabited by tourists who have almost submerged the Polynesian heritage. But both islands owe their distinct beauty, power, and mystery to their origins in volcanic fire.

8
Lava, Ash,
and Bombs

70 Pahoehoe lava flow, Hawaii. (Photograph by U.S. Geological Survey.)

A blast of burning sand pours out in whirling clouds.
Conspiring in their power, the rushing vapours
Carry up mountain blocks, black ash, and dazzling fire.

—LUCILIUS JUNIOR (A.D. 50)

. . . .

Volcanoes are dark windows to the interior of the Earth. Because their products are the only direct samples of the composition of the Earth's deeper levels, the aspect of volcanology that studies these materials has received considerable attention. Clues left behind in successive layers of volcanic rubble help describe the character and sequence of prehistoric eruptions, and provide a broader picture of volcanic events than historic activity can.

Most people think that lava flows are the only products spewed forth from volcanoes, but actually volcanic ash and larger solid fragments, called volcanic cinders and blocks, form the major products of observed eruptions. Lumping together all the sizes of solid fragments, geologists call this volcanic debris *pyroclastics*, which literally means fire fragments. Pyroclastics derive from three sources: magma that is cooled and broken into fragments by expanding gases at the moment of eruption; fragments of old crater walls that are ripped loose in explosive eruptions; and clots of liquid lava thrown into the air that cool during their flight.

Pyroclastic rocks are classified by the general size of the fragments. Volcanic dust is as fine as flour; volcanic ash is more gritty, with particles up to the size of rice; cinders include pieces as big as golf balls; and blocks cover everything up to chunks the size of a house. Volcanic bomb is a special term for a block-sized clot of liquid lava thrown from an erupting vent (Figure 71). The brilliant arcs on time-lapse

71   A large volcanic bomb from Mauna Kea Volcano, Hawaii. This
50-kilogram specimen shows the twisted flow lines often acquired
while these globs of hot plastic lava are spinning in flight. Pencil at
bottom shows scale.

photographs of volcanic eruptions are the traces of volcanic
bombs in flight.

Pyroclastic rocks are erupted in two different ways: either
as *airfall deposits* or as *pyroclastic flows.* Explosive volcanic
eruptions often hurl fragments to great heights, and as the
debris falls back to Earth it forms a distinct layer that blan-
kets the slopes of the land. The falling process allows for

72 Volcanic ash layers in a road cut on Oshima Volcano, Japan. Airfall material is characterized by distinct layers that follow the slopes of the ground surface on which they fell. Two generations of ashfalls are seen here separated by an erosional surface. The beds are not folded; the inclined layers are the original attitude in which they accumulated.

some sorting of the debris; the coarser fragments fall first and nearby, while the dust is winnowed away to fall last, sometimes at great distances. Airfall deposits can be recognized by this layering and sorting (Figure 72).

Sometimes explosive eruptions produce a cloud of volcanic debris so charged with fragments that it is too heavy to rise. This emulsion of gas and fragments forms a glowing avalanche or nuée ardente, the most dangerous kind of volcanic hazard. Glowing avalanches travel up to 100 kilometers per hour, and flatten and burn most everything in their paths, as they did at Mont Pelée (mentioned in Chapter 5). Small glowing avalanches often flow down the valleys on a volcano's flanks, but larger masses expelled at high speeds, or accelerated by steep slopes, can sweep over small hills or across large flat areas in their path. Glowing avalanche deposits pile up in low-lying areas after the avalanche loses its speed. These pyroclastic flow deposits are distinct from airfall debris: they exhibit only vague layering and almost no sorting of the finer and coarser fragments. Roads cut in airfall deposits show a sharp banding of coarse and fine layers, often of different colors, while cuts in pyroclastic flows show massive deposits that look like pink or buff concrete.

The contrast in explosive debris around a volcano tells something of the nature of its previous eruptions and thus helps to predict the nature of possible future eruptions. For example, at Pompeii, the Roman city buried in volcanic ash from Vesuvius, the beginning of the A.D. 79 eruption produced several distinct layers of airfall deposits, but the upper layers of ash are more vague and have the character of pyroclastic flows. This would explain the relatively small number of bodies found buried at Pompeii; most people escaped during the early rain of ashes, but stragglers were smothered and buried by the later glowing avalanches (Figure 73).

In stream valleys near explosive volcanoes there are often terraces and banks of poorly sorted gravel in a matrix of fine silt. These are mudflow deposits. Sometimes mudflows occur when heavy rains wash down loose ash from earlier eruptions or clay from the deeply weathered rocks around fumaroles (volcanic gas vents) and hot springs. More often, though, they happen during an eruption that ejects a crater lake or that rapidly melts the snow and ice on a volcano's high summit. These huge floods of water surge down the volcano's flanks, picking up volcanic ash and soil, and quickly thickening into mudflows. The surging mud in turn picks up larger rocks and boulders, and the entire mass thunders down the valleys like a torrent of wet concrete.

73 Cast of a dead dog buried by volcanic ashes at Pompeii. During excavation, holes were found with skeletal remains inside. By carefully injecting the hole with plaster, a cast of the corpse is formed. About 2000 human victims have been unearthed at Pompeii. (Alinari/Editorial Photocolor Archives, Inc.)

The 1985 tragedy at Nevado del Ruiz Volcano in Colombia was entirely the result of mudflows (Figures 50 and 51). In 1845 an eruption or earthquake had triggered mudflows from Ruiz that killed about 1000 people, and the new town of Armero was built on top of the old flows. In the November 1985 eruption hot pyroclastic flows caused huge floods of meltwater mixed with ash to pour off the summit. Most of the water rushed down the tributaries of the Lagunillas River picking up soil, rocks, and trees as it swept along. In places these floods — now mudflows — scoured the canyon walls to heights of 80 meters above the normal stream levels.

The mudflows roared down the Lagunillas Valley at speeds of 40 to 60 kilometers per hour. The town of Armero was

located where the narrow canyon meets the wider, open valley of the Magdelena River. At the canyon mouth where the
torrents spilled out on Armero the mudflows were as much
as 30 meters high, but they quickly spread out to dense
floods 3 to 5 meters deep. Armero was swept away. The
deposit of dried mud left behind is about 1 meter thick and
covers an area of 40 square kilometers. Boulders as large as
10 meters lie scattered where the town once stood.

Geologists had warned the people of Armero about the
danger of mudflows if Ruiz erupted, and there was a 2-hour
period between the main summit eruption and the time the
mudflow reached them. But the townspeople of Armero
didn't know what a mudflow was; the summit of Ruiz was
not visible, and there was no flood warning device or system
set up in the canyon above Armero. In hindsight the tragedy
might have been prevented. In reality it was not.

Besides mudflows, large avalanches from steep flanks of
volcanoes pose an additional hazard. The deposits from these
debris avalanches form thick, hummocky piles of broken
rock in the valleys and plains surrounding some volcanoes
(Figure 34). Avalanches can be triggered by heavy rainfall or a
strong earthquake without a volcanic eruption. However, the
oversteepening of a slope already near failure by the injection
of a shallow plug of magma, as occurred at Mount St. Helens
in 1980, may be more common than was previously realized.

Horseshoe-shaped craters that formed where a combination of avalanche and explosion has torn out a whole sector
of a steep volcanic cone are now being recognized on several
active volcanoes. With knowledge gained from the Mount St.
Helens avalanche and eruption, geologists with the U.S. Geological Survey have finally solved the mystery of an extensive
area of hills and mounds of broken volcanic rock northwest
of Mount Shasta in California. They now believe that about
300,000 to 360,000 years ago a gigantic avalanche from an
ancestral peak of Mount Shasta rushed down the Shasta River
Valley for 43 kilometers. The avalanche deposit covers 450
square kilometers and has a volume of 26 cubic kilometers. It

is the largest landslide known to have occurred on the Earth during the last million years.

Avalanches and mudflows are more common on stratovolcanoes than on shield volcanoes. In addition, many stratovolcanoes have eruptions that begin with pyroclastic emissions and end with lava flows. This may be because there are higher concentrations of gas in the upper parts of magma chambers or because the shallow magma, erupted first, is cooler and more solid. No one is sure, for measurements of gas content and magma temperatures just prior to eruptions simply don't exist.

Oceanic-ridge volcanoes and Hawaiian volcanoes erupt mainly lava flows. If we count the unseen flows deep beneath the sea, lava becomes the major product of all of the Earth's volcanoes. Shallow submarine eruptions like Surtsey can build an island of volcanic ash, but the great volume from deeper eruptions goes into streams of underwater lava.

Individual lava flows are tonguelike in shape, much longer than they are wide. On the Island of Hawaii a typical lava flow might be 10 kilometers long, 200 meters wide, and 3 meters thick; but there is so much variation that any standard flow dimensions can be misleading. Each eruption covers only a small fraction of the island with a finger of lava. This finger forms a low ridge, and later flows will either run beside the ridge or between ridges formed by earlier eruptions. The process is like covering a jug with candle drippings; it takes hundreds of wax flows to build up a covering layer. The volcanic pile above sea level on the Island of Hawaii is the accumulation of literally hundreds of thousands of lava flows.

A lava flow is hypnotic to watch. There is often a central river of orange-red molten rock 5 to 10 meters across, flowing at speeds of 5 to 50 kilometers per hour depending on the slope. The flow then oozes out on all sides from this central stream and forms slowly advancing dark lobes of cooling lava rubble riding on a molten but unseen core of the flow. These lava blocks tumble down the steep front of the advancing flow, giving a glimpse of the glowing interior, and are slowly overridden by the advancing flow. The growing edges and fronts of the flow look like giant slow-motion bulldozer treads moving out, down, and under as the mass of the flow spreads forward. The perimeter of the dark, growing flow is much larger than the central river of glowing, fast-flowing lava (Figure 74).

In Hawaii, the kind of lava flow just described is called an *aa* flow, pronounced *áh ah*. Its major characteristic is the rubble of broken lava blocks on its surface. Adventurers with thick boots have walked on these rubble surfaces while the flows are still slowly moving, but aa flows are hard enough on boots after they have stopped and cooled.

Another kind of Hawaiian lava flow is called *pahoehoe*, pronounced *pa hóy hoy*. These flows are generally thinner than the aa flows and form a smooth to wrinkled surface of solid rock (Figure 70). Old Hawaiian foot trails favor the ancient pahoehoe flows and for good reason. Bare feet will last for many more kilometers on their smoother, more solid surfaces (Table 1 and Figure 75).

Sometimes lava rivers crust over and form tunnels filled with fast moving streams of lava. As an eruption wanes, the lava in these tunnels drains out, leaving empty caves known as lava tubes within the cooled flows. These tubes are 1 to 10 meters in diameter; some can be followed underground for hundreds of meters.

The barren, smooth surfaces of pahoehoe flows compared to the rubble that forms aa flows are so distinctive that the Icelanders also have two separate words — *helluhraun* for pahoehoe and *apalhraun* for aa — to describe them where they occur in Iceland. The largest lava flow of historic record was an aa (apalhraun) flow that issued from a 25-kilometer-long fissure in Iceland from June to November 1783. Called the Laki flow, it covered more than 500 square kilometers with lava, completely filling two deep river valleys in the process. The volume of lava produced by the Laki fissure during several months of eruption was 12 cubic kilometers, enough to fill Yosemite Valley to a depth of 300 meters (Figure 76).

74 Flowing basalt lavas, especially aa, often have central channels that move at several kilometers per hour. These channels are red-hot (in this photograph light gray) in contrast to the partly cooled, black margins of the flow that advance more slowly, at rates of several meters per hour. (Photograph of the 1977 eruption of Piton de la Fournaise on Reunion Island by Pierre Vincent.)

TABLE 1
Forms of volcanic products

Form	Name	Characteristics (dimensions)
Gas	Fume	
Liquid	*Lavas*	
	Aa	rough, blocky surface
	Pahoehoe	smooth to ropy surface
Solid	*Airfall fragments*	
	dust	$<\frac{1}{16}$ mm
	ash	$\frac{1}{16} - 2$ mm
	cinders	$2 - 64$ mm
	blocks	>64 mm solid
	bombs	>64 mm plastic
	Pyroclastic flows	flows fluidized by hot gases
	Mudflows	flows fluidized by rainfall, melting ice and snow, or ejected crater lakes
	Avalanches	Thick, hummocky deposits of broken rock

The texture of lava and volcanic ash is largely controlled by the number and size of gas bubble holes in the rock. Pumice is one extreme, being mostly holes. This frozen glass froth is so light that pieces of it float on water. Dense, solid rock without holes is the other extreme, and is less common than pumice. Most volcanic rocks are somewhere in between (Figure 77).

Magma is a melt of silicate compounds of variable composition. The common elements in the melt are oxygen, silicon, aluminum, iron, calcium, magnesium, sodium, titanium, and potassium. Silica, the compound of one silicon and two oxygen atoms (SiO_2), is the most abundant constituent; alumina (Al_2O_3) is second. The proportion of silica varies from about 45 to 78 percent of the total. Various types of magma and

75 Lava flows of aa (left) and pahoehoe both issued from Kilauea Volcano in Hawaii in 1973. The dark, rough aa is about 3 to 4 meters thick; it was covering the smoother, glistening pahoehoe when the flow stopped.

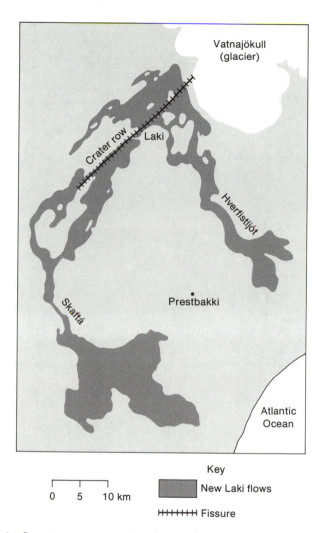

76 Laki flow in south-central Iceland. The 1783 eruption from a
25-kilometer-long fissure produced 565 square kilometers (12 cubic
kilometers) of basaltic lava flows, a world record. (Map data from
Sigurdur Thorarinsson.)

TABLE 2
Types of igneous rock

Range of SiO_2 content	Extrusive (erupted on surface)	Intrusive (solidified below surface)
45–54%	basalt	gabbro
54–62%	andesite	diorite
62–70%	dacite	granodiorite
70–78%	rhyolite	granite

their resultant igneous rocks are classified by their silica content.

Geologists enjoy naming rocks, and there are hundreds of varieties. However, most volcanic rocks fall into one of four clans: basalt, andesite, dacite, or rhyolite, which have a silica content of about 50 percent, 57 percent, 66 percent, and 74 percent. Rocks that contain more silica also contain more sodium and potassium and less iron, calcium, and magnesium. These last three elements, particularly the iron, form dark minerals, so that basalts are dark gray, almost black; andesites are medium gray; and dacites and rhyolites are light gray to tan. One important exception is obsidian, a glassy form of rhyolite once used for arrowheads. Obsidian is nearly black. Although there is less iron in rhyolite, in obsidian it is so finely divided into tiny crystals of opaque iron oxides that it makes the glass look shiny black (Table 2).

The chemistry of volcanic rocks is only part of the story of their complex composition. As magma cools, various min-

77 Basaltic lava is often filled with gas bubble holes formed when steam and other gases dissolved in the magma are released by the low pressures at the Earth's surface. Tops of flows usually have more trapped bubble holes (vesicles) than the centers of flows. The small crystals are olivine, one of the first minerals to form from the cooling melt. (Photograph at true scale by James Griggs, U.S. Geological Survey.)

erals start to crystallize from the melt. Crystallization takes time. If the magma cools rapidly, within seconds or minutes, the compounds do not have time to arrange themselves into minerals, and the result is a dark, opaque glass. If the magma cools more slowly, within days or years, the minerals have time to form and grow.

The cooling of molten basalt in Kilauea Iki lava lake in Hawaii is a good example of volcanic rock formation. The lava was erupted in 1959 at temperatures up to 1200°C, and was nearly all liquid except for a few percent of small olivine crystals. Most of the water and other gases dissolved in the magma were vaporized and lost in the fume from the fire fountains, as the lava welled out of the vent and ponded in an older crater. The surface of the lake cooled quickly and formed a glassy crust with many bubble holes. The deeper crust formed more slowly because of the insulating effect of the overlying crust, and crystals of various minerals began to appear. Since olivine crystallized first, at temperatures from 1250 to 1190°C, some crystals were present at the time of eruption. Pyroxene formed next at temperatures between 1190 and 1180°C, and then plagioclase feldspar at 1170 to 1160°C. By the time the temperature had dropped to 1065°C the basalt was half liquid and half crystals of plagioclase, pyroxene, and olivine, and had become hard enough so that steel probes could not be pushed into this mixture at the bottom of shallow drill holes. Magnetite began to crystallize at 1030°C, forming black mineral grains that give the basalt much of its dark color. By 980°C the basalt was all crystals except for 5 to 10 percent glass. It was still red hot, but had effectively become a solid.

During cooling and crystallization, the composition of each mineral is quite different from the overall composition of the original magma. This differentiation keeps changing the composition of the remaining melt fraction as crystallization becomes more complete (Figure 78). The most evident effect is in the composition of the final interstitial glass by the time cooling has reached 980°C. That glass has a silica

78   Photomicrograph of a very thin slice of Hawaiian basalt from
Kilauea Iki lava lake. Drilling core-holes into the slowly cooling lake
provides samples of "quick-frozen" basalt in which the drilling water
suddenly chills the slowly cooling melt and arrests the process of
crystallization. The large crystal on the right is olivine and the
smaller, sticklike crystals are feldspar. The uniform gray area
surrounding the silicate crystals is glass formed from the sudden
cooling of the melt. (Photograph by the U.S. Geological Survey.)

content of 60 percent, compared to 48 percent in the original
melt.

The cooling of andesite and rhyolite magma is equally
complex, and other silicate minerals including quartz become
important constituents of their crystallization into volcanic
rocks. The important difference between rocks formed from
a cooling silicate magma and ice formed by cooling water is
the mixture of minerals in igneous rocks. Water freezes at
0°C and forms only one mineral; magma freezes from 1250
down to 700°C and there are two or three, or more, minerals
in the final solid rock.

The volumes of lava and pyroclastic rocks produced in individual historic eruptions range from a few cubic meters up to 50 cubic kilometers. On the average, subduction zone volcanoes produce about 1 cubic kilometer of new volcanic rock each year, composed mostly of pyroclastics.

The volume of volcanic rocks produced by the oceanic-ridge volcanoes is largely hidden in the deep oceans, but it can be estimated indirectly. The spreading rates and sizes of the plates are reasonably well established and these data allow an estimate of the new area of seafloor that must be created every year to fill in the opening cracks between the spreading plates; the figure is about 2.5 square kilometers per year. Allowing 0.5 to 1 kilometer for the average thickness of the basalt flows that form the seafloor, the average amount of oceanic ridge eruptive products is about 1 to 2 cubic kilometers per year.

Hawaiian volcanoes average about 0.1 cubic kilometer per year of basalt lava flows, but the total for all hot-spot volcanoes is difficult to estimate because of the long intervals between eruptions in places like Yellowstone. A reasonable guess is an average of 0.5 cubic kilometer per year for the volcanic products of hot spots. The Earth's present volcanoes thus have a total output of about 3 cubic kilometers of new rock each year on the average. Many years go by without large volcanic eruptions, and then a Krakatau-type eruption comes along to catch up on the lag. In addition to the erupted rocks, shallow injections of magma intruded and crystallized beneath volcanoes also amount to large volumes, perhaps as much or more than the erupted rocks.

Huge deposits of pyroclastic flows that cover thousands of square kilometers and are tens to hundreds of meters thick exist in Japan, New Zealand, Central America, the western United States, and many other volcanic regions of the world. Some of these deposits give every indication that they were poured out in a single enormous eruption that would dwarf Krakatau and Katmai. The volume in these deposits is on the order of 100 to 1000 cubic kilometers compared to the 30 cubic kilometers of Katmai. This raises some fundamental questions. Was prehistoric volcanism, say a million years ago, greater than it is now? Or is the time span of recorded volcanic eruptions so short, about 200 years, that the data we have cover too short a time to be representative? We think the latter is true. Krakatau and Katmai are probably only small samples of what nature can deliver in the way of volcanic cataclysms.

9
Cones and Craters

79 Pavlof and Pavlof's Sister, stratovolcanoes in the Aleutian Islands, Alaska. (Photograph by Katia Krafft.)

Only to a magician is the world forever fluid, infinitely
mutable and eternally new. Only he knows the secret
of change, only he knows truly that all things are
crouched in eagerness to become something else, and it
is from this universal tension that he draws his power.

—PETER BEAGLE (1976)

. . . .

Mountains come in different
styles. Some, like the Himalayas, form where the crust of the
continents is telescoped together by powerful compressive
forces. Others, like the ranges between the Rockies and the
Sierra Nevada, form by the down faulting of keystone blocks
as the crust pulls apart under tension. Still others, such as the
Appalachians, result from regional uplift and the subsequent
etching by erosion of hard and soft rock formations — folded
by earlier compression — to form ridges and valleys.

Volcanoes are a mountain style all their own. They are
built upon the landscape by outpouring of new rock. Their
forms change rapidly, some even during a person's lifetime.
In the Tolbachik region of Kamchatka, a new cinder cone
grew to a height of 600 meters in just four months in 1975.

Geologists learn that the hills are not everlasting, that
erosion slowly strips away the mountains and fills the inter-
vening basins with their debris. It is usually taken for granted
these days that river valleys were carved out by the streams
they contain. But move to an active volcanic terrain and all
the rules change. The mountains are growing, new rocks are
forming, and the valleys are often the spaces between lava
flows. In other words, some valleys were not formed by
erosion, but by lack of construction. Even experienced geolo-

gists must remind themselves that they are in a strange land where the rules are often reversed.

Volcanoes form some of the most beautiful and unusual landscapes on Earth. Their power and fire command respect and remind one of the intense vitality of our Earth. *Kazan*, the Japanese word for volcano, means fire mountain; our word *volcano* is the name of an island near Italy whose volcanic peak was considered the forge of Vulcan, the Roman god of weapons.

Volcanic mountains have shapes that range from the perfect cones of Mount Fuji in Japan and Mayon in the Philippines to flat lava plateaus in Iceland that barely meet the designation of mountain. Their craters range from vast circular basins called calderas, several kilometers in diameter, to tiny vents a few meters across (Figure 80). Several factors are at work in producing these great variations in form.

The shape of the vent from which the volcanic products escape to the surface is of prime importance. It is usually a long, nearly vertical crack in the ground, several hundreds to thousands of meters long and deep, and only a few meters wide. Magma rises through this fracture and issues along a linear vent at the surface. The Laki eruption in Iceland and the beginning of the Puu Oo eruption in Hawaii are examples of eruptions from linear vents.

A specific location along a linear vent often becomes the major source of volcanic emissions as an eruption progresses, forming a central vent from which a volcanic mountain begins to grow. If a volcano is eroded down to its roots, the chilled magma in the exposed feeding cracks is seen as long, low ridges with greater resistance to erosion. These features are called volcanic dikes. The eroded remnant of a steep pipelike conduit that feeds a central vent is called a volcanic neck (Figure 81).

The viscosity of the magma as it erupts also has a profound impact on the shape of volcanoes. Very viscous lavas form a steep-sided plug over the vent called a lava dome. Solid fragments thrown from a vent form a pile of debris around or downwind from the crater called a cinder cone (Figure 40).

80 Summit of Cotopaxi Volcano, Ecuador. The nested craters result from explosive eruptions of different intensities. Snow and ice dominate the summit of this 5900-meter peak despite its volcanic activity and its location less than one degree south of the equator. (Photograph by G. E. Lewis, U.S. Geological Survey.)

These cones have very straight sides with slopes of about 30°, the angle of repose above which the cinders will slide until the stable angle is established. Very fluid lavas, on the other hand, flow long distances on gentle slopes, forming lava plateaus or low-sloping volcanic piles called shield volcanoes. Since the composition of a lava is generally related to its viscosity — basalt is more fluid and rhyolite more viscous — the shape of a volcano is often an important clue to its composition.

81 Ship Rock in New Mexico is a volcanic neck with radiating
dikes. Erosion has stripped away the volcanic cone, leaving only the
hard skeletal remains. Ship Rock is 450 meters high and the dikes
form great walls stretching across the desert. (Photograph from
Geology Illustrated, by John S. Shelton, p. 15. W. H. Freeman and
Company, Copyright © 1966.)

Many explosive volcanoes begin an eruption with volcanic
ash followed by lava flows. The alternation of ash and flows
forms the steep concave slopes of the classic volcanic cone.
The scientific name for this type of structure is stratovolcano, or composite cone, because of the layering of pyroclastic deposits and lava flows (Figures 82, 83, and 84).

The surface environment of the volcanic vent also has a
major effect on the shape of the resulting volcano. Submarine
volcanoes are the best examples of the effects of environmental factors. As explained in Chapter 3, deep submarine volcanoes are not explosive because the water pressure is so great

82 Mayon Volcano, Philippines, in eruption. The rising ash column and descending nuée ardente partly conceal the perfect symmetry of Mayon's stratovolcano cone. (Photograph by Dainty Studio, Daraga, Albay, Philippines, April 30, 1968.)

83 Initial stages of an explosion cloud forming on Lassen Peak in California. This stratovolcano with a summit lava dome erupted from 1914 to 1917. (Photograph by B. F. Loomis, June 14, 1914, courtesy of the National Park Service.)

84 Santiago Crater of Masaya Volcano in Nicaragua reveals the
inner structure of a stratovolcano. The light layers are lava flows and
the dark layers are ashfalls. The thick dark layer at the top is part of
a cinder cone whose summit is just to the left of this photograph.

that steam cannot form and expand. However, the water chills the lava faster than the air would, so the lava piles are generally more steepsided than those same lavas would be if they were erupted above water. Shallow submarine eruptions are usually explosive, even when they involve basalt magma that would be poured out in relatively quiet fountains and flows on land.

Volcanic eruptions beneath thick piles of glacial ice show many of the same features as submarine eruptions: deep out-pourings of pillow lava, followed by shallow-water explosions of volcanic debris, and capped by gently sloping flows of lava that reached above the glacial surface. The table mountain volcanoes of Iceland are thought to have originated in this way (Figure 85). The glacial ice caps are now largely

85 Herdubreid, a table mountain in Iceland. Pillow lava on the steep flanks covered by gently sloping flows on the summit indicates that table mountains were formed by eruptions beneath a glacial ice cap. The elevation to the edge of the table marks the thickness of the ice. (Photograph by Gudmundur Sigvaldason).

gone, but the steep shoulders on table mountains mark their former thickness.

Other factors such as the volume of erupted material and the length of time between eruptions also influence the form of a volcano. Small volumes of pyroclastic flows fill valleys, while huge pyroclastic flows form plateaus that bury all the underlying topography. Los Alamos, New Mexico, is located on a volcanic plateau formed about 1 million years ago (Figure 86). Plateaus of pyroclastic flow material are common in many volcanic regions of the world. Fortunately, none have formed in historic time. Their great size and speed of emplacement would be cataclysmic.

The craters on volcanoes are also formed in many ways. Funnel-shaped craters usually result from an initial enlargement of the vent by volcanic explosions followed by the collapse of loose debris back into the crater at the end of the eruption. After gas escapes from magma, the reduction in volume sometimes allows the magma to drain back down the vent, forming a deep cylindrical crater on the volcano's summit. The escape of magma from a vent on a volcano's flank can also cause subsidence of the summit crater. The crater on Mount Fuji is about 700 meters in diameter and 100 meters deep with nearly vertical walls.

Craters are sometimes filled with domes of viscous lava; Lassen Peak in California is an example. Rows of small craters along a fissure erupting fluid lava can be buried by the thick flows that issue from them. The lack of cones and craters on extensive lava plateaus such as the Columbia River lava fields in Washington and Oregon makes it difficult to locate the actual vents from which the lavas erupted.

When a volcano erupts a very large volume of magma, the void created underground cannot support itself and part of the volcano subsides, or collapses, into the emptied space. The collapse creates a large circular basin with steep walls, sometimes several hundred meters high; many such basins are the remains of the summit of an earlier volcanic cone. Collapse calderas form within a few hours or days, as at Krakatau, and are generally associated with great eruptions.

86 Los Alamos, New Mexico, the birthplace of nuclear power, lies
on the flank of a giant prehistoric volcano. The city sprawls across a
canyon-cut plateau of thick ash-flow deposits, erupted about 1
million years ago. Ejection of this huge volume of ash caused the
volcanic summit to collapse forming Valle Grande, the 20-kilometer-
diameter caldera covered by grasslands in the background.
(Photograph by William Regan of the Los Alamos Scientific Laboratory.)

The caldera at Valle Grande, just west of Los Alamos, is 20 kilometers in diameter and about 1 kilometer deep. It apparently resulted from the sudden collapse associated with the 300 cubic kilometers of ash flows that violently erupted and formed the pyroclastic plateaus that surround the caldera. Crater Lake in Oregon is another collapse caldera. It formed during a great eruption that occurred about 7000 years ago, as dated by the carbon 14 in the trees incinerated to charcoal beneath the pyroclastic flows.

Calderas also form on Hawaiian volcanoes. The summit of the major shield volcano Mauna Loa is the rim of a large elliptical caldera 3 by 5 kilometers in diameter with vertical walls up to 200 meters high (Figure 87). This caldera formed 600 to 700 years ago, and the absence of explosive volcanic debris around its rim indicates that it formed by the collapse associated with a major removal of magma from its summit chamber. Large flank eruptions of lava are thought to have caused the magma removal and caldera collapse.

Craters and calderas are difficult to tell apart, and in fact Kilauea Caldera is often called Kilauea Crater, even on official maps. A practical though arbitrary distinction can be made on the basis of size. Craters are smaller than 1 kilometer in diameter; calderas are larger than 1 kilometer in diameter. In addition, calderas are generally formed by collapse (Color Plate 23), while craters may form by either collapse or explosion.

Volcanic mountains evolve through time; their mature and old-age forms are far from simple. A cinder cone is often the early stage of a stratovolcano. Caldera collapse may then swallow up the summit of a large stratovolcano, and new lava domes may subsequently appear over vents along the rim of the caldera. One way out of this classification dilemma is to call the result a complex volcano. Even so, with careful geologic mapping it is often possible to distinguish the component parts of a complex volcano and the order in which they formed. The history of eruptive habits and their sequence can be very useful in attempting to forecast the future hazards at a particular volcano (Figure 88).

87 Circular craters and a large 3-by-5-kilometer caldera indent the snow-covered summit of Mauna Loa Volcano in Hawaii. These collapse features with cliffs up to 200 meters high lie at an elevation of about 4000 meters, at the top of a huge gently sloping shield volcano. Historic eruptions have been filling the craters and caldera with numerous flows. The view is to the north. (Photograph by the U.S. Army Airforce in 1939; courtesy of the National Archives.)

Volcanoes can be erupting, dormant, or dead. Their life-times are extremely variable. The great volcanic complex of the Valle Grande has been erupting intermittently for 15 million years. Most individual volcanoes in Iceland erupt only once, suggesting that Surtsey's lifetime was only 3½ years. An average life span for a recurrently erupting volcano is roughly 1 million years. In the end, erosion takes over and the stumps of vanquished volcanoes join the other passive mountains of the world.

88   Aerial view of Tongariro, Ngauruhoe, and Ruapehu volcanoes in New Zealand. The crater of Tongariro, in the foreground, is 1.3 kilometers wide and is transitional between a large crater and a small caldera. It is filled by ponded prehistoric flows cut by a small collapse crater. The cone of Ngauruhoe, in the middle ground, is typical of an active stratovolcano with a summit crater. Ruapehu, in the background, is also an active stratovolcano, but it contains a crater lake whose eruptions have prematurely eroded the volcano's flanks. (Photograph by S. N. Beatus, New Zealand Geological Survey.)

89   Mount Rainier, a massive stratovolcano in the Cascade Range of Washington. Several valley glaciers fed by heavy snowfalls have begun to erode this 4392-meter active volcano. (Photograph by Norman Bishop, National Park Service.)

The time of death can be estimated from the degree of erosion, but such estimates must be made with caution. Erosion itself is extremely variable: fast in humid climates; slower in cold, dry regions. In Hawaii there are vast climatic changes over short distances. The low slopes facing the trade winds are hot and humid and sustain more than 5 meters of rainfall per year. On the summit of Mauna Loa it is cold and relatively dry, and on the lee shore of Hawaii the climate is that of a desert. Lava flows only 50 years old have been reclaimed to soil and jungle in the hot, humid areas, while flows 1000 years old high on Mauna Loa look freshly erupted. In the high deserts of Mexico, cinder cones remain almost untouched by erosion for thousands of years.

But climates change and the tooth of time finally wears down all volcanoes. Since its formation a million years ago, half of the Los Alamos plateau has been incised by deep canyons. Islands like Hawaii are washed completely away by the sea in 5 to 10 million years, and then slowly subside beneath a growing coral atoll cap.

We have records of volcanic activity for 2000 years in Europe, 1000 years in Iceland, and only a little more than 100 years in the northwestern United States. Comparing this with a million-year volcanic life span and a similar time to erode away the dead cones and craters, it is folly to declare a volcano extinct just because it has had no historic eruptions. Any volcanic peak that shows little of the ravages of time, such as Mount Rainier, Mount Hood, or Mount Shasta, is only dormant (Figure 89).

10
Roots of Volcanoes

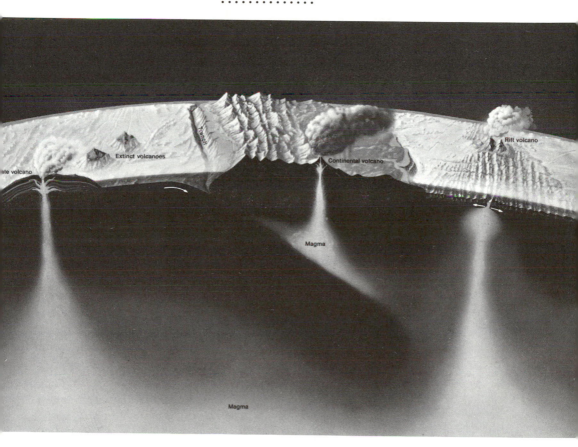

90 Schematic diagram of the three types of volcanoes related to plate tectonic processes. *Right:* Rift volcanoes formed by separating plates such as submarine volcanoes on the Mid-Atlantic Ridge and Icelandic volcanoes. *Center:* Volcanoes formed by converging plates at subduction zones such as Japan and the Andes Mountains of South America. *Left:* Hot-spot volcanoes such as Hawaii and the Hawaiian Ridge. (From *Powers of Nature.* Copyright © 1978, National Geographic Society. All rights reserved.)

Men argue, Nature acts.
—VOLTAIRE (1694–1778)

. . . .

Whe John Wesley Powell was
trying to establish the U.S. Geological Survey, the senator
from Nebraska challenged Powell by saying, "You can't see
any farther into the Earth than any other man." Even today
geologists can hardly deny the truth of this statement, but we
do have a great deal of indirect data on the inside of the Earth
that helps to guide our speculations.

For example, we can study the seismic waves from large
earthquakes because they travel through the Earth to seismographs around the entire globe. Earthquake waves change in
character as they travel away from their source; but regardless of the location of the earthquake, seismographic record-
ings made at equal distances from the source are remarkably
the same. This result can only be explained by an interior
structure of the Earth that is symmetrical about the center
(Figure 91). Thus if the Earth's interior is composed of various materials, they must be arranged in layers or spherical
shells like an onion.

We also have clues to the weight of the Earth's interior.
We know the average density of the whole Earth from the
magnitude of the force of gravity at the surface; it amounts to
5.5 grams per cubic centimeter, which is twice the density of
surface rocks. Therefore, some parts of the Earth's interior
must be very dense material to bring the average up to 5.5.

Reasonable speculations on the roots of volcanoes must be
consistent with our knowledge of the physics and chemistry
of the whole Earth as well as with our observations on the

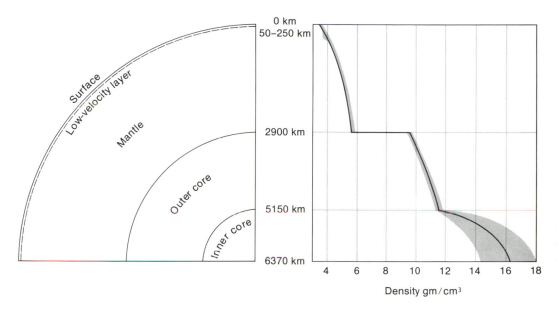

91 Estimated density of the interior of the Earth. The solid line in the graph on the right shows the most probable value of density at each depth, and the shaded region outlines the range of uncertainty. (Data from K. E. Bullen, "The Interior of the Earth." Copyright © 1955, by Scientific American, Inc. All rights reserved.)

surface geology. One fact is quite clear: the surface geology indicates that our Earth is very complex and heterogeneous. However, the physical and chemical data on the Earth's interior yield average values rather than details, so most models of the Earth's interior show simple shells of rock or molten metals of homogeneous composition. As a first approximation these cartoons are probably right, but the details are missing. Filling in this picture is the most fascinating challenge in geoscience research today.

These details are not trivial. Diamond and graphite are the same chemical, but wars have been fought over their difference. Synthetic diamonds can be made from graphite with complex high-pressure, high-temperature furnaces reaching ranges of 100,000 atmospheres at more than 1000°C. Natural diamonds occur in volcanic pipes that have originated at depths as much as 200 kilometers beneath the surface; thus the diamonds, their inclusions, and the pieces of wall rock erupted with them provide a direct sample of the composition, pressure, and temperature at depths in the Earth far below the reach of drilling (Figure 92).

Uplift and erosion of ancient volcanoes expose their shallow roots that were once as much as 10 kilometers below the surface. Postmortems on these rocks show that the dikes and pipes of chilled magma often connected surface vents to larger storage chambers of molten rock at depths of 2 to 10 kilometers beneath the surface (Figure 93). These shallow magma chambers were complex bodies of intersecting dikes and layers of molten rock, or sometimes more cylindrical masses called stocks or plutons. Their composition, the tex-

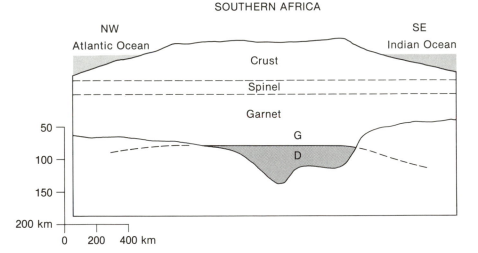

92 Schematic cross section through southern Africa based on inclusions brought up in diamond pipes and other volcanic pipes in which diamonds are absent. Spinel and garnet are characteristic minerals of the depth ranges indicated. The boundary labeled G/D is the transition between graphite and diamonds. (Modified from Francis R. Boyd, Carnegie Institution, Year Book 1986, p. 98.)

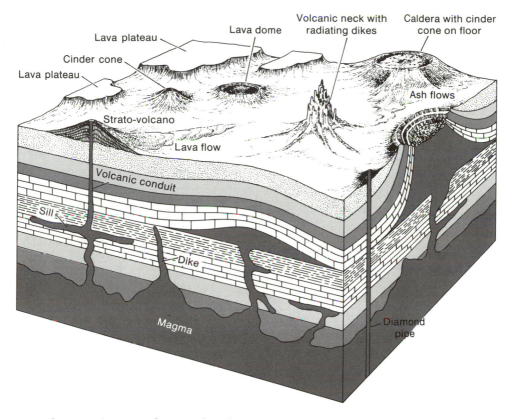

93 Schematic diagram of the surface forms and subsurface structure of various volcanic features. (After R. G. Schmidt and H. R. Shaw, *Atlas of Volcanic Phenomena*, U.S. Geological Survey, 1972.)

ture of their crystals, and the host rocks at their edges yield important clues to how the magma chambers were emplaced, and how and when they cooled into crystalline rocks. In general, the composition of shallow magma chambers is the same as that of surface volcanic products, but their texture is more coarsely crystalline because they cooled more slowly. For example, granite is the root rock in stocks beneath volcanoes that once erupted rhyolite lava flows or huge volumes of rhyolitic pyroclastic flows (Table 2, page 135).

However, shallow magma chambers are not the deep roots of volcanoes. They occur at depths too shallow for rocks to be melted by the Earth's heat. Uplift and erosion have not exposed the deep roots of volcanoes; they are still hidden from direct observation so our information about them is more tenuous. The sources of the heat that melts rocks are still under lively debate. The leading contenders include the Earth's original heat from the time of formation; heat from the breakdown of the radioactive isotopes of uranium, thorium, and potassium; heat from the gravitative energy of redistributing heavy elements toward the center of the Earth; and heat from the tidal friction of slowing the Earth's rotation.

The accretion of the planets at the time of formation of the solar system generated immense amounts of heat from collision and gravitational collapse. Whether the planets actually melted or not depends on the speed of their accretion, with rapid formation favoring higher temperatures. However, even if the original Earth were molten, the heat of formation alone cannot account for the estimated heat lost from the Earth over its 4.5-billion-year life span.

Moreover, even if the Earth had formed cold, the radioactive decay of unstable atoms would have started a warming trend — warming fast at first because of many short-lived, highly radioactive elements, and then more slowly from the longer-lived but less radioactive elements such as uranium 238, thorium 232, and potassium 40. The heat generated from the estimated remainder of these three isotopes in the Earth today can account for all of the world's presently escaping heat (Table 3).

As the primitive Earth was initially being heated by radioactive decay, melting and the gravitational segregation of iron to form the core would have greatly speeded the heating process, perhaps melting the entire Earth. Even so, this gravitational melting would have been a one-shot process and its heat long gone unless sustained by other processes.

The heat produced by tidal friction gets its energy from the slowing down of the Earth's rotation. (Some studies on the

TABLE 3
Radioactive heat production from uranium, thorium, and potassium
in common igneous rocks

Rock	Amount of radioactive element in rock (parts per million)			Amount of heat produced (joules/kilogram year)
	Uranium	Thorium	Potassium	
Granite	4	13	4	.03
Basalt	0.5	2	1.5	.005
Peridotite	0.02	0.06	0.02	.0001

growth bands of 400-million-year-old fossil corals indicate that a year may once have had more than 400 days.) Much of this energy is dissipated in the swirling tides of the Earth's oceans, but some geologists believe that the tidal warping of weak zones inside the solid Earth may be another continuing source of heat.

As in many geologic debates, the problem is complicated by too many plausible explanations. Probably more than one of the various theoretical sources of energy are involved, and all of them are virtually inexhaustible in terms of human time spans.

Regardless of the exact source of the heat in the Earth, much is known about the variation of temperature near the surface. In deep mines and drill holes, the temperature increases with depth. The rate of increase, called the thermal gradient, averages about 30°C per kilometer of depth. By measuring the heat-insulating quality of rocks, which is quite high, the actual loss of heat from inside the Earth can be calculated. This quantity is about 5000 times less than the heat that reaches the Earth from the sun. Even so, it is an enormous amount of energy, much larger than the more spectacular heat loss from all of the Earth's volcanoes.

At 30°C per kilometer the 800-to-1200°C melting temperatures of rock should be reached at depths of 30 to 40 kilometers beneath the Earth's surface. However, there is good evidence that the thermal gradient is not steady, but rather that the rate of increase slows at greater depths. This is because of the way the radioactive isotopes of uranium, thorium, and potassium are distributed within the Earth. These elements have an affinity to granitic rocks and tend to be concentrated in the Earth's crust. The production of heat from their radioactive decay therefore diminishes with depth, and this reduces the rate at which temperatures increase with depth. The best estimates of this effect indicate that temperatures inside the Earth reach 800 to 1200°C at depths of 60 to 100 kilometers beneath the surface. This is the same depth as the top of the seismic low-velocity layer described in Chapter 1 — an important point of independent evidence supporting the temperature calculations. The roots of volcanoes must then extend down at least 60 to 100 kilometers beneath the surface to reach a source of magma (Figure 94).

Seismic evidence indicates that the low-velocity layer is not a zone of completely liquid melt. Rather, the rock is only partially molten; perhaps a few percent of the total material is liquid and is contained in a spongelike mass of weak but solid rock at high temperature. How then does the magma separate and ascend toward the surface?

The density of magma is less than that of the rock from which it melts. Under the influence of gravity the lighter molten rock tends to rise, and the residual solid rock to sink. Any fractures reaching deep into the Earth would hasten this upward movement of magma, which would tend to escape in the same manner as petroleum gushes from a wild well. The problem is the conduit. Do fractures reach down through the rigid crust into the melt zone, or do bodies of magma push and melt their way slowly upward as great rising blobs to feed the shallow magma chambers? (See Figure 95.)

Separating plate margins have major fractures, and volcanoes along the mid-ocean ridges probably have conduits along these fractures between the plates. In these rift zones the thermal gradients are much higher than average, and

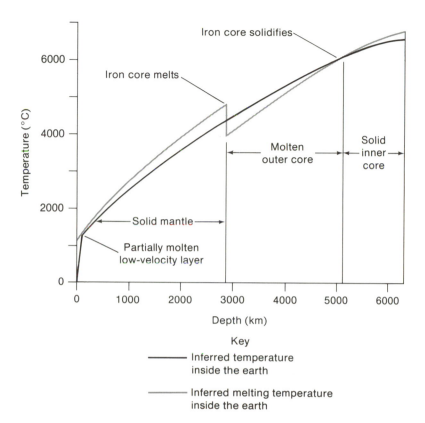

94 Graph of inferred temperature (black line) and inferred melting temperature (gray line) inside the Earth. There are four control points for this graph: (1) The thermal gradient near the Earth's surface is about a 30°C increase per kilometer of depth. (2) At a depth of about 100 kilometers the actual temperature and melting temperature curves must almost touch to account for the low strength and partial melting of the low-velocity layer. (3) For the lower mantle to be solid and the upper outer core molten, the actual temperature and melting temperature curves must cross. (4) For the lower outer core to be molten and the upper inner core to be solid, the actual temperature and melting temperature curves must again cross. (Data from J. Verhoogen, D. L. Anderson, G. Kennedy, G. Higgins, R. Jeanloz, and T. Ahrens.)

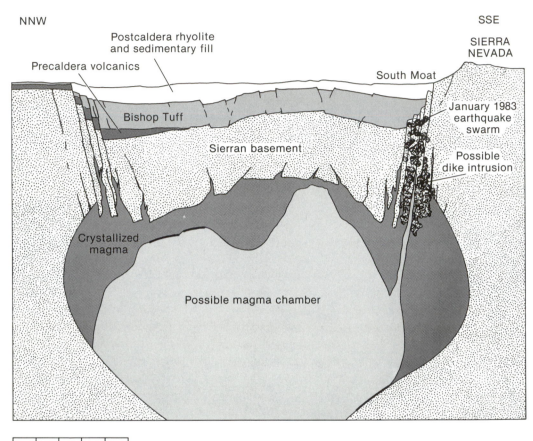

NNW

Postcaldera rhyolite
and sedimentary fill

Precaldera volcanics

SSE

SIERRA
NEVADA

South Moat

Bishop Tuff

January 1983
earthquake
swarm

Sierran basement

Possible
dike intrusion

Crystallized
magma

Possible magma chamber

0   1   2   3   4   5 km

No vertical exaggeration

95   Schematic cross section through Long Valley Caldera near
Mammoth Lakes, California. This caldera formed when 600 cubic
kilometers of pyroclastic flows called the Bishop Tuff were erupted
about 700,000 years ago. The most recent eruptions, 500 to 600
years ago, emplaced a north-south line of rhyolite domes in and north
of the caldera. Earthquake swarms and 40 centimeters of uplift
within the caldera from 1980 to 1983 indicated a probable injection
of new magma beneath the area. (After D. P. Hill, R. A. Bailey, and
A. S. Ryall, *Journal of Geophysical Research* 90, 1985, pp. 11111–
20 and cover.)

seismic evidence indicates that the low-velocity layer comes up to within 10 or 20 kilometers of the surface.

In island arc volcanoes at converging plate margins, the volcanoes occur in belts parallel to the marginal thrust faults but are offset about 150 kilometers onto the overriding plate. It is not clear if this location is a special fracture zone along which magma can ascend, or if the extra magma generated along the thrust surface forces its own way upward (Figures 90 and 96).

In Hawaii the location of earthquakes below the shallow magma chamber of Kilauea indicates that there is a zone of fractures shaped like an inverted funnel about 5 to 50 kilometers in diameter and from 10 to 50 kilometers deep, reaching down to the top of the low-velocity layer. The shape of this region of active cracking does not imply a major fracture zone parallel to the Hawaiian Island Chain, but rather a local zone of failure closely associated with the ascending magma. Here it appears that the magma forces its own way up to the shallow magma chamber beneath Kilauea. The rate of inflation of the summit area over the past 30 years indicates that magma is being fed continuously from depth into the magma chamber at 3 to 6 kilometers below the surface, at rates of about 100,000 to 500,000 cubic meters per day.

No one has ever seen the deep roots of volcanoes, but improved geophysical techniques can provide some startling indirect views. In Yellowstone Park, small delays in the transit time of vibrations from distant earthquakes indicate that a large body of magma or very hot rock underlies much of the region. By recording these delays of only a few seconds at many seismograph locations, geophysicists can map the rough size and shape of the huge thermal anomaly (Figure 97).

Another seismic technique, a spin-off from prospecting for oil by the reflections of sound waves generated at the surface, extends the "x-ray vision" of geophysicists to a depth of 50 kilometers. Analysis of the deep seismic cross sections obtained by this technique reveals a great deal of complexity in

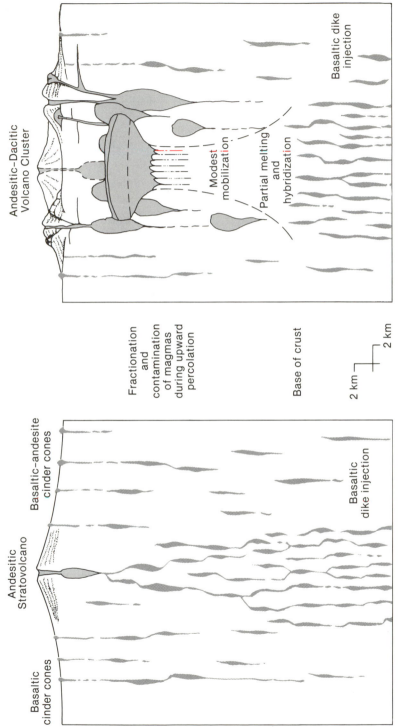

96 Schematic cross sections of an andesitic stratovolcano and an andesitic-to-dacitic complex volcano. Basalt is the primary magma rising from depth, but it becomes more silica rich by removal of early-formed crystals (fractionation) and by contamination of the basalt with crustal rocks of higher silica content. Andesitic to dacitic magma chambers are shown by the dotted pattern. (From Wes Hildreth, *Journal of Geophysical Research*, 86, 1981, p. 10179.)

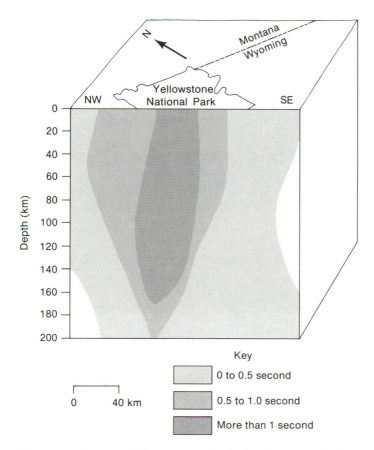

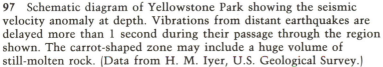

Key

0 to 0.5 second

0.5 to 1.0 second

More than 1 second

97 Schematic diagram of Yellowstone Park showing the seismic velocity anomaly at depth. Vibrations from distant earthquakes are delayed more than 1 second during their passage through the region shown. The carrot-shaped zone may include a huge volume of still-molten rock. (Data from H. M. Iyer, U.S. Geological Survey.)

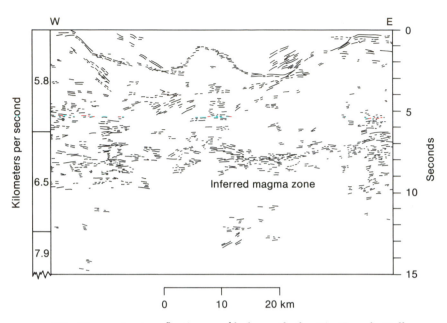

98 Deep seismic-reflection profile beneath the Rio Grande Valley near Socorro, New Mexico. The short lines indicate the apparent distance down to layers that echo strong vibrations generated at the surface. The left-hand scale shows the velocity of the seismic waves in kilometers per second. The right-hand scale shows the time delay between the signal and the echo. The base of the sedimentary rocks filling the valley is shown by the line of reflections at delay times of 1 to 3 seconds (depths of 3 to 6 kilometers). The zone of reflections with about 7 seconds delay time (depth 20 kilometers) is interpreted to be the top of a layer of molten rock. (After S. Schilt and others, *Reviews of Geophysics and Space Physics* 17, 1979, p. 359. Copyright © 1979, American Geophysical Union. All rights reserved.)

the rock structures at depth. In the Rio Grande Rift section in New Mexico, a major sound-reflecting zone at about 20 kilometers beneath the surface is thought to be a layer of magma (Figure 98).

For geologists and volcanologists who are getting their first geophysical look at magma, these are exciting times.

11

Origin of
the Sea and Air

99 Sea, steam, and flying rocks: Hawaiian lava flow enters the ocean. (Photograph by G. A. Macdonald, U.S. Geological Survey.)

The smell of sulphur is strong,
but not unpleasant for a sinner.

—MARK TWAIN (1866)

. . . .

The brimstone smell of sulfur dioxide at active volcanoes is noxious, especially to people with respiratory problems, but usually not fatal. However, another gas commonly exhaled at volcanic vents is more insidious. Carbon dioxide, a colorless, odorless gas, is heavier than air and can accumulate into concentrations that may suffocate animals and people with little or no warning. A tragic example of this occurred at Lake Nyos in Cameroon, West Africa, on August 21, 1986.

Lake Nyos fills a 1- to 2-kilometer-wide, 200-meter-deep crater on a dormant volcano that had not erupted in recorded history. Without warning a rumbling burst of gas, mostly carbon dioxide, belched from the lake and poured into the valley below. A survivor who lived above the lake heard the rumbling and in the darkening evening sky saw the gas cloud as a smoking river moving down into the valley. He felt a blast of wind from the lake and was gagged by its awful smell.

The dense cloud of gas, later estimated to have a volume as much as 1 cubic kilometer, flowed down the valley below the crater for 10 kilometers, killing 1700 people and 3000 cattle. Houses and farms were undamaged, but dead bodies were everywhere.

Scientists investigating the disaster agree that carbon dioxide gas of magmatic or volcanic origin was the killer, though they disagree about how it happened. Most of them think that magmatic gases had apparently been seeping into the lake from below for hundreds of years, and were dissolved and concentrated in the deep water near the lake bottom by the high pressure of the overlying water. This rare phenomenon can occur in a tropical lake because the warm, less-dense layer of water near the surface prevents overturn of the lake water, which would release most of the gases dissolved at depth. In temperate regions cooling of the surface water in winter eliminates the density layers, and wind and currents can bring the deep water to the surface so any accumulated gas is released harmlessly.

Once the deep water in a tropical crater lake has become saturated with carbon dioxide, the potential for its rapid effervescence — like the sudden opening of a champagne bottle — exists.

Although most scientists agree up to this point, they disagree on what triggered the sudden release of dissolved gas. Some feel that large amounts of cool rainwater entering Lake Nyos, or a landslide on the steep wall of the lake basin, may have triggered the gas release. Once the effervescence was started it would stir the lake and continue the rapid degassing. Another school of thought is that a small volcanic eruption beneath the lake triggered the gas outburst, and a few investigators believe that all the carbon dioxide was of sudden eruptive origin. No new volcanic rock has been found around the lake, but evidence for this interpretation may lie hidden at the bottom of now calm Lake Nyos.

In a larger view, volcanic gases over geologic time have helped to make the Earth, with its abundant surface water, a special planet in our solar system.

Of all the inner planets — Mercury, Venus, Earth, and Mars — only the Earth has oceans. Venus has a massive, dense atmosphere of carbon dioxide and sulphuric acid that hides its rocky face in perpetual clouds, but its 500°C surface temperature is too hot to allow the condensation of an ocean.

What is the origin of the water and gases on the Earth, and why are the inner planets so diverse in this respect? Many factors seem to be involved: distance from the sun, the composition of the nebular gases from which the planet condensed, the mass of the planet, the presence or absence of an original atmosphere, the changing temperature of the interior of the planet, and the amount of water and other gases bound up with the rocks and metals that form the planet.

The distance from the sun strongly affects a planet's surface temperature, and the mass of the planet controls its field of gravity. Light gases escape into space when the surface is warm and the gravity low. The moon's surface is a vacuum for these reasons; it does not have enough mass to hold an atmosphere at its distance from the sun.

The question of how much of the Earth's atmosphere was there originally—that is, formed at the time the planet formed—is the basis of a controversial and lively debate also involving the role of volcanoes. If the Earth formed slowly by accretion from a nebular dust cloud, it may have remained cool enough for an original atmosphere to form. By contrast, if there was rapid hot accretion or if surface temperatures were higher than at present because of either internal processes such as radioactive heating or external processes such as excessive heat from the early ignition of the sun, any original atmosphere would have boiled away.

The "neon argument" supports the concept of loss or lack of any original atmosphere. Neon is an inert gas; it does not combine with silicate minerals or metals to form solid compounds. Neon is also relatively abundant as a gas in the cosmos, and its physical properties indicate that it is not subject to loss into space from the Earth's present atmosphere. Any original atmosphere of the Earth derived from a cosmic dust cloud should have had a modest amount of neon in it. But the Earth's present atmosphere has only a trivial fraction of neon, much less than that expected in an original atmosphere. The lack of neon indicates that the original neon was lost along with all the other gases and water from the hot surface of a primitive Earth. A later atmosphere and oceans evolving from volcanic gases escaping to the Earth's surface would not include neon. Only gases such as water, carbon dioxide, and others that could be chemically bound into solid matter would be released by melting and eruption on the Earth's surface.

For these reasons, many geologists think that part of the Earth's oceans and atmosphere has been boiled out of the Earth's interior, particularly during the period of melting from gravitational energy as its dense core formed. However, collisions with the abundant icy comets that are inferred to have populated the early solar system may have been the major contributor of water and carbon dioxide to the young Earth's surface.

Before the concept of plate tectonics was firmly established, it was thought that volcanic gases were the major source of the Earth's oceans and atmosphere, and that this was a long evolutionary process. Now the concept has shifted, and volcanoes are viewed as recycling the oceans and atmosphere, instead of creating them. The general argument goes like this: water, carbon dioxide (in calcium carbonate sediments), and other volatile compounds are carried down into the mantle on seafloor crust at subduction zones. After a few million years these volatiles are exhaled by eruption at subduction zone volcanoes; or after a few hundred million years by eruption at rift volcanoes. Hot-spot volcanoes may also recycle some of the volatiles incorporated into the low-velocity layer at subduction zones, but the ratio of helium isotopes in hot-spot volcanic gases suggests that they have a deeper, more primitive source.

With this concept in mind, let's look at the actual data on gases escaping at active volcanoes. Molten basalt rising to the Earth's surface contains about 0.5 percent by weight of dissolved gases. These gases are in solution in the same way that carbon dioxide gas is dissolved in beer. They exsolve and effervesce into gas bubbles and foam as the magma reaches the surface, just as beer foams when its pressure is suddenly released.

It is not easy to determine the composition of volcanic gases, since they escape during eruptions. Huge volumes of gases are involved in explosive eruptions, but it is virtually impossible to get close enough to sample them before they mix and react with unknown amounts of air (Figure 100). Indirect methods of sampling have proved more successful. Gases in deep submarine eruptions are frozen into the glassy rinds of pillow lava. These trapped gases have been analyzed by several investigators and provide some of the best estimates of the composition of volcanic gases currently available.

Sometimes crystals forming in a cooling magma chamber will enclose a tiny pocket of melt. If these crystals are erupted, the melt pocket quenches to an inclusion of glass in which the volcanic gases are trapped. Analysis of these inclusions by Fred Anderson at the University of Chicago has revealed that subduction volcanoes have a much higher gas content than submarine rift volcanoes.

Richard Stoiber of Dartmouth College has pioneered still other techniques for analyzing volcanic gases. He uses instruments called absorption spectrometers to measure the sulfur dioxide in volcanic fume clouds backlighted by the sky; he also analyzes gases adsorbed on volcanic ash particles collected as they fall from the eruption clouds. His studies indicate that each active volcano generates about as much sulfur gas pollution as a major coal-fired electric power station.

Recent study and analysis of the submarine hot springs occurring along mid-ocean ridges indicate that they are also major sources of volcanic gases, especially carbon dioxide.

The sum of these studies allows some reasonable estimates of the volume and composition of the volcanic gases currently being added to the water and air budget of the Earth. By numbers of atoms, hydrogen is the most important constituent of volcanic gas followed by oxygen, carbon, sulfur, chlorine, and nitrogen. As the elements combine at the surface conditions on the Earth they become water, carbon dioxide, sulfur dioxide, hydrochloric acid, and nitrogen. The ratios of these volcanic gases are in good accord with the ratios of water, carbon, chlorine, and nitrogen in the air, oceans, and surficial rocks of the Earth. However, the ratio of sulfur is not.

100   Volcanic gases escaping from this crack in a cinder cone
formed during an eruption of Kilauea Volcano in Hawaii are
depositing an encrustation of minerals. Wayne Ault of the Hawaiian
Volcano Observatory measures the temperature of the vent and
collects gas for chemical analysis. (Photograph by the U.S. Geological
Survey.)

Although the compositional ratios appear generally correct for a volcanic recycling of the Earth's air and water, what about the total amounts of these gases?

Figure 101 shows a comparison of volatile elements and compounds in the Earth's oceans, sedimentary rocks, and atmosphere compared to their volcanic production. From the recycling point of view, this comparison indicates that about 25 percent of the water, chlorine, and nitrogen in the Earth's atmosphere has been reworked by subduction and volcanic eruption, and about 75 percent of the carbon has been recycled.

The data in Figure 101 are still being refined; the total abundances of water, chlorine, carbon, and nitrogen are fairly well established, but sulfur in the top layers of the oceanic crust is not included. The volcanic exhalations are only first approximations, and it is not known if the current rate of volcanic activity is representative of average volcanism throughout geologic time. Nevertheless, a comparison based on approximate data can be important for qualitative purposes even though future data may refute its quantitative conclusions. In other words, the present data support the concept of recycling, though the total amount of various volatiles that have been recycled is still uncertain.

Sulfur appears to be a special problem. At the present rate of emission from volcanoes, there should be 50 times more sulfur at the Earth's surface. What has saved us from the sulfuric acid blanket that plagues the planet Venus? The answer is probably iron sulfide — the common mineral pyrite, or "fool's gold" — and also the plate tectonic process. Instead of being released into the ocean or atmosphere, sulfur reacts with iron and forms insoluble iron sulfide, which stays in the oceanic crust and is returned via a subduction zone to the shallow interior of the Earth.

The probability that sulfur is scavenged from the Earth's surface by the seafloor-spreading machine has spawned a new school of thought championed by William Fyfe of the University of Western Ontario in Canada. Fyfe points out that perhaps more water is being consumed in the water-rich

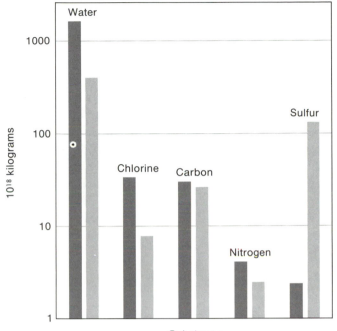

101 Comparison of volatile molecules and elements in the Earth's oceans and atmosphere to their volcanic production. (Note logarithmic scale.) For each substance, the bar on the left represents the total weight of that material in the air, oceans, and sedimentary rocks of the Earth. The bar on the right represents the weight of that same substance currently being produced from volcanoes multiplied by the age of the Earth. It is apparent that some process such as subduction must remove sulfur from the Earth's surface.

rocks entering subduction zones than is being returned to the surface in volcanic gases.

This idea reverses the older concept that the Earth has been releasing gases to the surface throughout geologic time. In this new view, a primitive Earth had a thick atmosphere and universal ocean that covered solid rocks of low water and gas content. The stirring of this Earth by plate tectonics caused the surface water and gases to mix down into the mantle rocks, perhaps scrubbing out the excess sulfur in the process.

If the water that still covers most of our world's surface was not originally part of the Earth, it must have been added early from outside. Comets, made largely of ice, are likely candidates for this extraterrestrial source. Apparently comets still collide with the Earth occasionally, and during the early days of the solar system the number of comets and their collisions are inferred to have been much more frequent.

If comets and not volcanoes provided most of the Earth's early sea and air, volcanologists can no longer claim that these essentials of life were born of fire. Nevertheless, recycling is an important task, especially if the overall process can clear the air of sulfuric acid. Ongoing volcanism and tectonism have helped to provide the long-term balance among land, sea, air, and climate that has been essential to the evolution of life on Earth.

12

Volcanic Power

102   Wairakei geothermal field generates electrical power in New Zealand.

Fires that shook me once, but now to silent
ashes fall'n away
Cold upon the dead volcano sleeps the gleam of
dying day.

—Alfred, Lord Tennyson (1809–1892)

. . . .

Geothermal energy was a phrase known to only a few specialists until the 1974 energy crisis. Now, although not exactly a household name, it has become a familiar term for an alternative source of energy.

In discussing geothermal energy and power, it is important to understand the subtle difference between these terms. Heat is a form of energy, and there is an immense amount of it inside the Earth. For each kilometer of depth the temperature increases about 20 to 60°C, depending on the region (Figure 103). The heat energy contained in just the upper 10 kilometers of the United States is estimated to be 3.3×10^{25} joules. If it were accessible, it would supply our energy needs for the next 100,000 years.

But potential energy becomes practical only when it can be consumed at some useful rate. Power is a measure of the *rate* at which energy is made available or is consumed. Energy is measured in joules. Power is measured in joules per second or watts. There is plenty of diffuse energy in the Earth; turning it into useful power is the critical problem.

The difference between energy and power becomes clear in the following examples: The amount of solar energy is enormous, but the solar power reaching the Earth is modest —averaging about 40 watts for each square meter of surface. A lightning bolt contains only a modest amount of energy,

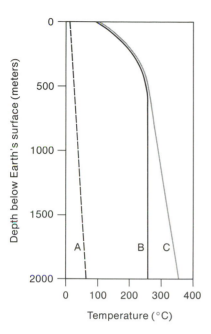

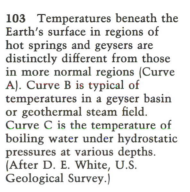

103 Temperatures beneath the Earth's surface in regions of hot springs and geysers are distinctly different from those in more normal regions (Curve A). Curve B is typical of temperatures in a geyser basin or geothermal steam field. Curve C is the temperature of boiling water under hydrostatic pressures at various depths. (After D. E. White, U.S. Geological Survey.)

equal to that of about 2 barrels of crude oil, but it expends this energy in a fraction of a second, unleashing enormous power.

Volcanic explosions are often compared to nuclear bomb blasts, but the analogy is misleading. Although the heat and mechanical energy in the 1883 eruption of Krakatau was in the order of 5000 megatons of TNT, this energy was released in a series of explosions lasting almost a day. A nuclear bomb goes off in a single almost instantaneous flash, unleashing power in amounts unmatched by geological phenomena.

Geothermal energy, like solar energy, is enormous, but its natural rate of release is trivial—averaging about $\frac{1}{16}$ watt from beneath each square meter of the Earth's surface. Even if geothermal energy could be converted to electricity with an efficiency of 20 percent, it would require all of the heat flow from an area as large as a football field to power a

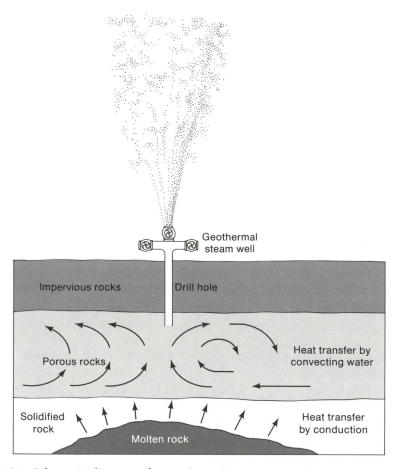

104   Schematic diagram of a geothermal power reservoir.

60-watt light bulb. Only in a few volcanic regions like Yellowstone, New Zealand, and Iceland, where geysers and hot springs are abundant, does nature sustain a significant output of geothermal power (Figure 102 and Color Plates 14 and 25).

For geothermal power to be practical, some special situation must exist that can concentrate the Earth's heat energy into a small area. Natural or artificial underground reservoirs of steam or hot water that can be funneled into a drill hole provide this special situation (Figure 104).

In nonvolcanic areas, drill holes to depths of 4 or 5 kilometers may reach temperatures near 100°C. However, in young volcanic regions, where molten rock has brought heat up from deeper levels, it is possible to drill into rocks and steam reservoirs heated to 100 to 350°C or hotter at depths of 1 to 3 kilometers. To develop the true potential of geothermal power it is necessary to locate these shallow bodies of hot rocks and fluids, and to tap their pent-up energy with a system of drill holes.

Exploring for geothermal power is similar to exploring for oil, except that the geologic setting is volcanic rather than sedimentary. Most of the existing high-temperature geothermal power fields have been found in active or young volcanic regions.

The form of heat transfer in a given region is of key importance. Heat is transferred by radiation, conduction, and convection. Radiation transfers a significant amount of heat through transparent media like air and space, but it is much less effective in solids. Conduction is such a slow process in good thermal insulators like rocks that only small amounts of heat are transferred inside the Earth by conduction. The very slow release of the Earth's interior heat through its surface (averaging 0.06 watt per square meter) is controlled by this slow conduction process.

Convection is the only process rapid enough to transfer the Earth's heat at rates sufficient to produce significant power. Convection involves the actual physical movement of molten rocks or hot fluids, generally upward, because these hot rocks and fluids are less dense than their surrounding cooler media (Figure 105).

Geothermal power fields occur where magma has moved upward from depths of 50 to 100 kilometers and brought the high temperatures (900 to 1200°C) of these depths to near the surface. Groundwater heated by these volcanic intrusions can form another convection circuit bringing hot springs and geysers to the very surface, or remaining sealed below the surface awaiting the wildcatter's drill.

Geothermal prospects related to volcanic activity are of three types: hydrothermal reservoirs, hot dry rocks, and

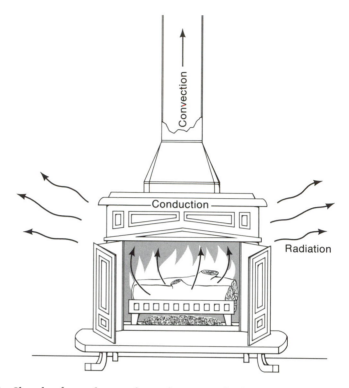

105 Sketch of woodstove shows heat transfer by convection of the heated air and wood smoke in the stove; by conduction through the firebrick and iron walls of the stove; and by radiation from the surface of the stove through the open space of the room.

magma reservoirs. Of the three, hydrothermal reservoirs are the easiest to develop because their hot water and steam are waiting to be tapped (Figure 106).

Larderello, Italy, is an area of natural hot springs. The boric acid concentrated in these thermal waters has been extracted for more than 200 years. Wells drilled to increase chemical production encountered steam, and were first used to produce electricity in 1904. Some 300 wells to depths of 300 to 700 meters have been drilled over the years and have outlined a producing steam reservoir at 235°C and 30 bars of

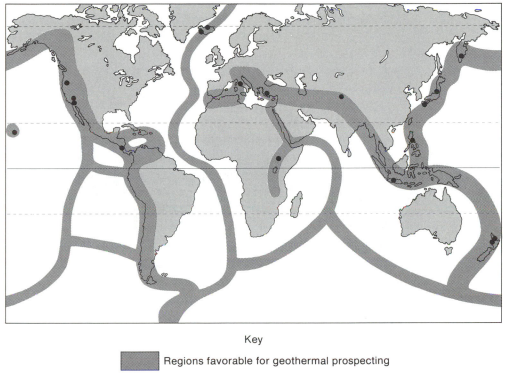

Key

Regions favorable for geothermal prospecting

• Location of geothermal power plants

106   Map of geothermal regions of the world. Notice the close relationship to zones of active volcanoes.

pressure. The reservoir is in porous limestone, but young volcanic rocks in the area are considered to be the heat source. The field has produced some 400 megawatts of power for the last 40 years and is still going strong (Figure 107).

Icelanders began to drill for hot water and steam in 1925. By now they have developed more than 250 fields whose power is used mainly for space heating. Some 70 percent of Reykjavík, the capital city of nearly 100,000 people, gets its heat and hot water from 110 wells, 300 to 2200 meters deep, that tap water at about 100°C in porous basalts. Although

107   Larderello, Italy, is the site of the world's first geothermal steam field. Started in 1904, it now produces about 300 to 400 megawatts of electricity. The huge chimneys are cooling towers similar to those used at nuclear power plants for recycling the cooling water. (Photograph by Patrick Muffler, U.S. Geological Survey.)

once flowing wells now need to be pumped, the temperatures have shown little decrease. For the people in oil-barren, arctic Iceland, geothermal power is the very life blood of their warmth and comfort (Figure 108).

The Geysers, California, a region of young volcanic rocks in the Coast Range of California north of San Francisco, was drilled for steam in 1921. Electricity was first generated in 1959 and the power field has been steadily expanded since then. More than 300 wells, 500 to 2600 meters deep, produce steam at about 240°C and 30 bars of pressure from a reser-

108 *Geysir* is an Icelandic word meaning to gush, but the Great
Geysir of Haukadalur, the world's original, seldom performs. Its
small neighbor, Strokkur Geysir, seen in this photograph, erupts
every few minutes.

voir of fractured shaley sandstone. The production has been
expanded to nearly 2000 megawatts, enough electricity for a
city of 2 million people. The largest geothermal electrical
generating installation in the world (Figure 109), the Geysers

109 The Geysers, California, once a hot-spring health spa, is now the world's largest geothermal steam field. Producing nearly 2000 megawatts, the field generates enough electricity to supply a city of 2 million people. (Photograph by Pacific Gas and Electric Company.)

is an exceptionally valuable geothermal field; the power produced there is low cost and relatively trouble free, making it the shining light of geothermal prospectors.

On the Island of Hawaii, a recently drilled geothermal exploration well has encountered some of the hottest underground fluids yet found. Drilled into lava flows on the east rift of Kilauea Volcano to a depth of 1969 meters, the hole has a bottom temperature of 350°C. This well has been generating about 2 to 3 megawatts of electricity since 1982

(Figure 110). Additional wells have been drilled nearby, and a 25-megawatt generating plant is planned.

The prospects for generating geothermal power from hot dry rocks are more speculative. These potential fields involve areas of higher-than-normal thermal gradients on the order of 60°C per kilometer of depth in areas of impermeable rocks. Drill holes to 3- or 4-kilometer depths can reach down into these hot dry rocks. Artificial fractures are established between two closely spaced holes and cold surface water is pumped down an injection well. Heated by the hot rock

110 First geothermal steam well in Hawaii is located on the east rift of Kilauea Volcano. A 3-megawatt electrical generator has been installed on this well. (Photograph by Larry Kadooka, *Hawaii Tribune Herald*.)

along the fractures, it rises as hot water or steam in a return well (Figure 111).

Los Alamos Scientific Laboratory in New Mexico is actually performing this experiment on the flank of the Valles caldera. Cold water pumped down one 3-kilometer-deep well returns up another at 135°C. The key question not yet answered is the nature of the fractured rock at depth. If the cooling of the buried rock mass will lead to a volume reduction and more fracturing of still hot rocks, as the experimenters hope, then the wells may produce enough power for commercial use. By contrast, if no new cracks form, the original fractures will soon cool and the amount of power produced will decline too rapidly to pay for the drilling costs.

The process of artificially making a geothermal reservoir within hot buried rocks is a difficult and expensive experiment, but if successful, the potential is enormous. Much of the young mountain terrain in the western United States, as well as in Hawaii and Alaska, is of volcanic origin and forms a tempting but well-locked buried treasure of geothermal energy.

Even molten rock itself is a potential source of power. Magma contains about 1000 joules of heat energy per gram. The energy in 1 cubic kilometer of magma is enough to light San Francisco for 200 years. But tapping it requires truly advanced technology; although scientifically it is feasible to extract power directly from shallow bodies of magma beneath volcanic centers, the engineering technology is still years away.

Initial experiments conducted by drilling into buried masses of molten rock have been done on Kilauea Iki lava lake in Hawaii. This great lake of lava formed during an eruption of Kilauea Volcano in 1959, when lava flows ponded in an ancient crater to a depth of 100 meters. Lava is such a good insulator that holes drilled in 1979 deeper than 50 meters were still reaching partially molten rock in Kilauea Iki. Conventional rock drilling techniques using abundant water to keep the drill bit cool have been successful in reaching the molten rock. However, efforts to emplace devices

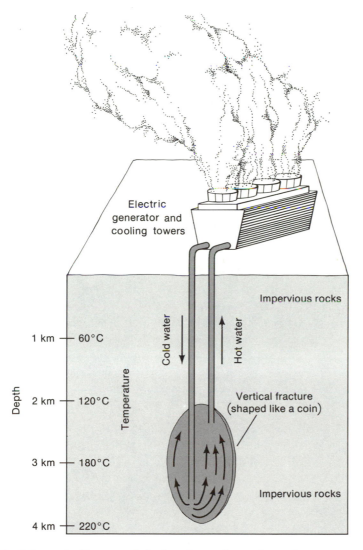

Electric generator and cooling towers

Impervious rocks

Cold water

Hot water

Depth

Temperature

1 km — 60°C

2 km — 120°C

Vertical fracture (shaped like a coin)

3 km — 180°C

Impervious rocks

4 km — 220°C

111 Schematic diagram of the hot dry rock geothermal power concept. Two holes are drilled into impervious rocks in regions where the temperature increases rapidly with depth. The holes are connected by hydraulic fracturing, a process of fracturing rock by pumping high fluid pressure down a well. Surface water is injected into one hole; it gets heated from contact with hot rocks at depth, and rises in the second hole as hot water or steam. Cooling of the rocks at depth causes further fracturing, allowing the circulating water to reach additional hot surfaces. Preliminary tests near Los Alamos, New Mexico, with wells drilled to a depth of 3 kilometers in granite at 200°C have been encouraging.

down the holes into the molten rock to determine the feasibility of extracting energy have not yet been successful.

Even though geothermal power is still an infant and largely unproved industry, its potential makes it worth serious effort and investment. The U.S. Geological Survey in a recent assessment of potential geothermal energy resources in the 50 states to depths of 10 kilometers listed the following estimates: hydrothermal reservoirs, 12×10^{21} joules, or

112 Old Faithful geyser in Yellowstone National Park has erupted every 40 to 80 minutes for the past 100 years. Spraying 50,000 kilograms of boiling water 35 to 50 meters high, each eruption releases about 1.9×10^8 joules of energy during its few minutes duration (about 1 megawatt of power). Thick deposits of silica precipitated from the cooling waters indicate that the Yellowstone geyser basins have been active for thousands of years.

about 2 times the energy in the world's oil reserves; hot dry rock, 32×10^{24} joules, or about 6000 times the energy in the world's oil reserves; magma reservoirs, 4×10^{23} joules, or about 80 times the energy in the world's oil reserves.

Volcanoes, directly and indirectly, are powerhouses of enormous potential. The most scenic, such as Yellowstone, Kilauea, and others in national parks, should never be developed (Figure 112). But others may help to provide light and warmth in centuries to come. It will take a major research and engineering effort involving much time, labor, and money to find out. Like all human adventures, high payoff involves high risk.

Plate 14 Eruption of a geyser in central Iceland. Geysir, an Icelandic word meaning to gush, is the original word for these spectacular spouting hot springs. Other noteworthy examples are found in Yellowstone National Park and near Rotorua in New Zealand.

Plate 15   Mount St. Helens in 1969, viewed from Spirit Lake. Before the massive eruption in 1980 the summit elevation of this beautiful stratovolcano was 2950 meters.

Plate 16   Mount St. Helens and Spirit Lake in 1982. The rim of the 2-kilometer-wide, horseshoe-shaped crater reaches an elevation of 2549 meters, and the crater bottom is more than 1000 meters below the pre-1980 summit elevation. The new lava dome can be seen inside the crater. (Photograph by Lyn Topinka, U.S. Geological Survey.)

Plate 17 Explosive eruption of Mount St. Helens on July 22, 1980. Although this explosion generated an ash cloud that reached a height of 18 kilometers, its energy was about 100 times less than the May 18, 1980 eruption. (Photograph by Katia Krafft.)

Plate 18 Lava erupting from a vent on the northeast rift zone of Mauna Loa Volcano in 1984 forms a 20-meter-wide river of fire. (Photograph by Katia Krafft.)

Plate 19 The main lava flow from Mauna Loa's 1984 eruption poured from a vent at 2900 meters and traveled 25 kilometers down the mountain in five days to an elevation of 900 meters, only 6 kilometers from the city of Hilo. (Photograph by David Little.)

Plate 20 A dome-shaped fountain of lava 20 meters high gushed for hours from the vent of an east-rift-zone eruption of Kilauea Volcano in 1969. (Photograph by J. B. Judd, U.S. Geological Survey.)

Plate 21 A fumarole (volcanic gas vent) in Kilauea Caldera deposits sulfur as the gases cool and mix with air. (Photograph by R. L. Christiansen, U.S. Geological Survey.)

Plate 22 Halemaumau Crater in Kilauea Caldera begins to fill with a lava lake during an eruption in 1961. (Photograph by L. R. McBride, U.S. National Park Service.)

Plate 23 Crater Lake National Park, Oregon. The lake, deepest in the United States, fills a 10-kilometer-wide caldera that was formed by the great eruption and collapse of Mount Mazama Volcano 6900 years ago.

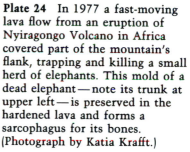

Plate 24 In 1977 a fast-moving lava flow from an eruption of Nyiragongo Volcano in Africa covered part of the mountain's flank, trapping and killing a small herd of elephants. This mold of a dead elephant—note its trunk at upper left—is preserved in the hardened lava and forms a sarcophagus for its bones. (Photograph by Katia Krafft.)

Plate 25 At Waimangu hot springs near Rotorua, New Zealand, terraces of silica are deposited as the water cools and precipitates its load of dissolved compounds. Most of the colors are formed by algae that thrive in the warm, nutrient-rich water.

Plate 26 Submarine hot springs have recently been discovered at many locations along the volcanic mid-ocean ridges. These "black smokers" at 13° North Latitude on the East Pacific Rise are pouring 350°C mineral-laden water into the cold, deep, bottom-water 2500 meters below sea level. Iron sulfide and other metallic sulfide particles precipitating in the suddenly chilled hot-spring water form the black "smoke." (Photograph by J. L. Cheminée, Observatoires Volcanologiques, Institut de Physique du Globe de Paris, doc. Ifremer; taken from the French submersible CYANA in 1982.)

13
Volcanic Treasures

113   Quartz vein in road cut, Mother Lode gold country near Mariposa, California.

But see the mountain
Shaking with the waves of heat
Where day has gone.

—ONITSURA (1661 – 1738)

. . . .

Volcanoes are nature's forges and stills where the elements of the Earth, both rare and common, are moved and sorted. Some elements are diluted and some pass through unchanged, but many are transported and concentrated into those precious lodes that people seek for fortune or industry.

Economically important elements concentrated directly by volcanic action, especially by the intrusion of magma bodies into the Earth's crust, include fluorine, sulfur, zinc, copper, lead, arsenic, tin, molybdenum, uranium, tungsten, silver, mercury, and gold. These concentrations are mainly formed as hydrothermal vein deposits, which are the mineral fillings precipitated from hot waters percolating along underground fractures. Veins generally consist of one or more common minerals, like quartz or calcite (calcium carbonate), in which the more precious minerals, like gold or galena (lead sulfide), are scattered as small specks or crystals.

Theoretically the process is simple, but in operation it can be enormously complex. Basically, the magmatic roots of volcanoes supply the heat source and perhaps some of the ingredients for a giant still. As the magma cools and the common silicate minerals crystallize to form basalt or granite, the water and other gases, as well as the rarer elements that don't fit into the rock-forming silicate minerals, become concentrated in the residual liquid magma. As the cooling reduces the volume of the rocks, they crack, allowing the hot residual magmatic fluids, rich in water and precious elements, to escape from their underground forge. During the ascent of these hydrothermal solutions toward the surface, cooling and decreasing pressure cause various minerals, both common and rare, to precipitate and form veins. Certain minerals precipitate over a large range of pressure and temperature and are common throughout the vein; others such as gold and silver may precipitate over a very narrow range of pressure and temperature to form localized bonanzas within the vein (Figure 114).

Veins are usually steeply inclined ledges dipping into the Earth, a few centimeters to many meters thick, and often many hundreds of meters or several kilometers in length (Figure 113). The gold-bearing veins of the Mother Lode sys-

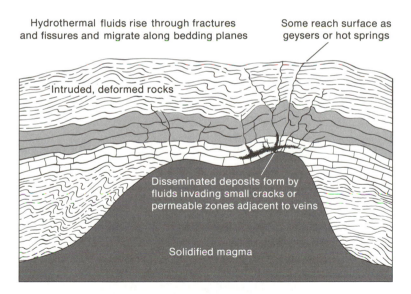

Hydrothermal fluids rise through fractures and fissures and migrate along bedding planes

Some reach surface as geysers or hot springs

Intruded, deformed rocks

Disseminated deposits form by fluids invading small cracks or permeable zones adjacent to veins

Solidified magma

114 Ore deposits are often found in close proximity to an intrusion of solidified magma. Many such deposits probably precipitate out of the hot waters associated with the cooling magma. (From F. Press and R. Siever, *Earth*, Second Edition, p. 577. W. H. Freeman and Company, Copyright © 1978.)

tem in the Sierra foothills of California trend north-south and dip steeply down toward the granite roots of the range. Although each vein is generally no more than a meter or so thick and a few kilometers long, the vein system crops out for more than 300 kilometers in the western Sierra Nevada. Hot waters escaping through steep cracks from the volcanic roots of the range deposited mainly hard, milky-white quartz in the veins, with few (but enough) specks of gold and pyrite (iron sulfide, or fool's gold) to start the rush to California.

The type of rock surrounding the cooling magma reservoir is of key importance in the formation of ore deposits. In Hawaii (in fact, in most oceanic volcanic islands) ore deposits are nearly nonexistent. Part of the reason for this may be that most oceanic islands are slowly sinking from their own enormous load, thus hiding any ore deposits that have formed. But even in the unusual case where uplift and erosion have exposed the roots of volcanic islands, hydrothermal ore deposits are rare or absent. Volcanic rocks richer in silica than basalt — for example, dacite and rhyolite — are more often associated with hydrothermal ore deposits. Many geologists believe that this is because the rocks surrounding the magmatic roots of volcanoes are the true source of the valuable elements found in hydrothermal veins. According to this view, the volcanic rocks act as a heat source that pumps existing groundwater into a giant circulating system. Cold waters, being heavier, move down and into the cooling volcanic rocks carrying trace quantities of valuable elements leached from the surrounding rocks. Heated by the cooling magma, they become less dense and rise into the fractured rocks above. Cooling and losing pressure again, they precipitate their quartz and precious ores into the veins forming above the volcanic hearth (Figure 115).

Mercury, copper, sulfur, and fluorine have been measured in volcanic gases in Hawaii, so there is no question that at least some of these elements originate directly in volcanoes. Gold, silver, and other valuable elements found in hydrothermal ore deposits may have to be preconcentrated in some earlier generation of continental crustal rocks before they can be reconcentrated by volcanic distillation.

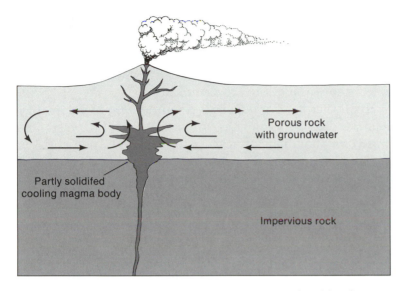

115 Schematic diagram of groundwater being circulated by the cooling of a magma body. The water seeps into the cooling magma body, is heated, and convects upward. Reaching cooler rocks above the magma body, the circulating groundwater also cools and precipitates vein minerals. The source of the minerals may be either the magma or the porous rock through which the groundwater circulates. In this model, the cooling magma body acts as a circulating pump and concentrator, rather than as a direct source of ore deposits.

Each mineral has its characteristic place in the hydrothermal system. Tungsten minerals precipitate at very high temperatures and often occur at the very point of contact between a chilled magma body and the rocks it has invaded, especially limestone. Scheelite, a calcium tungstate mineral, is brightly fluorescent under ultraviolet light. Tungsten prospectors seek out contacts between granite and limestone during the day, and then prospect these outcrops at night with "blacklights" to reveal the areas of high tungsten concentration.

Mercury is at the other extreme. Both as an element and in compounds, it is volatile; that is, it forms a gas at low temperatures and pressures. For this reason, much of the Earth's mercury is lost to the surface from volcanic steam vents and hot springs. Near many active volcanoes the concentration of mercury in the air exceeds the health standards established by environmental protection agencies. However, it is difficult to get the volcanoes to stop smoking.

Hydrothermal ore deposits in continental locations have been studied by geologists for more than 100 years, and mined for thousands of years before that. Only recently has the importance of submarine ore bodies deposited at mid-ocean rifts been recognized.

In the 1960s scientists probing into the floor of the Red Sea discovered some areas where hot but dense, highly saline bottom water overlies muds that are rich in iron, zinc, and copper minerals. Since the Red Sea is a volcanic rift zone, oceanographers suspected that the metal-rich sediments might have been precipitated from submarine hot springs.

Proof of this idea came in the late 1970s, when scientists in submersibles peered out on the strange landscapes of volcanic rift zones in the Eastern Pacific. Twenty-five-hundred meters below the surface, they were startled to see the "black smokers" we discussed in Chapter 3 — chimneys of iron, zinc, and copper sulfides a few meters high pouring out dark particles of iron sulfides. The water spouting from these chimneys was hot — 350°C — and as it was quickly chilled by the surrounding seawater, the dissolved metal sulfides precipitated into fine particles (the black smoke) or additions to the chimneys. Some of the metal sulfide deposits contain small but significant amounts of silver and gold. In addition to building the chimneys, the ore deposits form mats and crusts as thick as a few meters that spread over several hundred square meters around the vents.

The general model for the operation of these submarine hot springs and their attendant ore deposits is shown in Figure 116. Heat from the magma chamber beneath the rift zone drives a convective circulation of seawater within the porous basalts of the seafloor. Water sucked in on the rift flanks is heated and dissolves calcium, silica, and metallic sulfides, while depositing magnesium and sulfate. The heated dis-

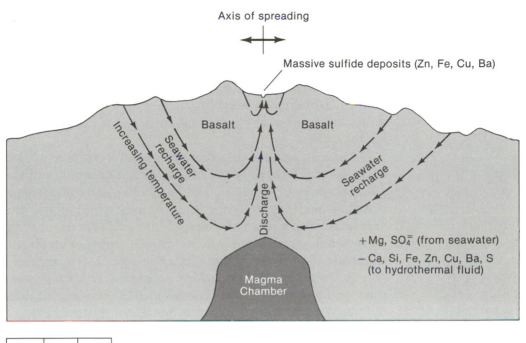

116 Schematic cross section of fluid circulation and hydrothermal deposits at submarine rift zone. Seafloor topography is exaggerated and depth to magma chamber is uncertain. (After R. A. Koski, U.S. Geological Survey.)

charge waters, with volcanic fluids rich in carbon dioxide and hydrogen sulfide, are cooled as they emerge on the seafloor and deposit their metal sulfides.

The large extent of submarine ore deposits is just now being realized. They apparently occur in many places along mid-ocean ridges, and as the seafloor spreads their areas increase. Although presently so deep they are out of reach of commercial mining, a few ancient deposits have been shoved up on land where oceanic plates have converged on continents. The metal sulfide mines in Cyprus and Japan, long puzzling to geologists, appear to have originated at submarine hot springs.

However, most ancient submarine ore deposits have probably been consumed in subduction zones as the ocean plates bearing them pushed beneath a continent. Perhaps they were and still are being recycled by subduction volcanoes into the more conventional hydrothermal ore deposits found in continental rocks.

Diamonds, perhaps the greatest mineral treasure of all, are also closely related to volcanic processes. Diamonds and the graphite cores of common pencils are the same element — carbon — but they are different minerals. In graphite, the carbon atoms are arranged in layers like mica sheets, and the loose bonding between layers permits the sheets to break and slide past one another. Graphite is therefore soft and greasy feeling. In diamonds, the atoms of carbon are compressed into a tight network that interlocks in all directions, forming the hardest substance known on the Earth (Figure 117). To attain this close packing of carbon atoms, extremely high pressures are needed — pressures that occur naturally only at depths of nearly 200 kilometers inside the Earth. Once formed, diamonds are stable at low pressures and temperatures; however, they will burn in air at high temperatures.

The right conditions to form diamonds apparently exist beneath the continents at a depth of nearly 200 kilometers and a temperature near that of molten rock. In fact, diamonds might not be all that rare if we could mine them at their deep source. Their occurrence at the Earth's surface results from a rare type of volcanic eruption that transports them rapidly from great depths into shallow vents called Kimberlite pipes (Figure 118). The reduction in pressure and temperature happens so rapidly that the diamonds do not revert to a more normal surface form of carbon such as graphite.

No one knows whether the type of volcano associated with diamond pipes is forming today. The peculiar Kimberlite volcanic rock and the presence of other minerals indicating that the volcanic fluids were extremely high in carbon

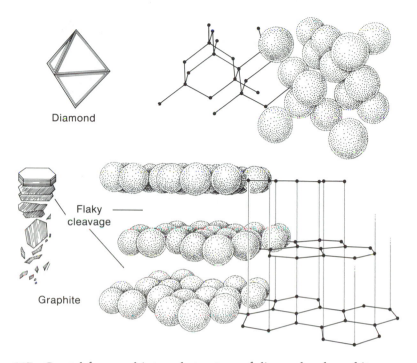

Diamond

Flaky
cleavage

Graphite

117 Crystal form and internal structure of diamond and graphite.
The three-dimensional network of atomic bonds in diamond makes
it extremely hard and durable. In contrast, the two-dimensional
network of major bonds in graphite makes it flaky and soft. (From
J. Gilluly, A. C. Waters, and A. O. Woodford, *Principles of
Geology*, Fourth Edition, p. 30. W. H. Freeman and Company,
Copyright © 1975.)

dioxide suggest an unusual kind of explosive volcanism that
may occur only during certain episodes of geologic history. A
few active volcanoes in East Africa, especially those whose
rocks are unusually high in carbon dioxide (like Ol Doinyo
Lengai), may be the closest active relatives to a diamond-pipe
volcano (Figure 119).

On a recent expedition to the summit of Ol Doinyo Lengai
scientists found small, active lava lakes in the crater. These
molten lavas had temperatures ranging from 500 to 550°C
and appeared to have very low viscosity. The exceptionally

A

118 *A.* Famous Kimberley
Diamond Pipe in South
Africa. This volcanic vent
was mined over 1000 meters
deep before 1908.
(Photograph by DeBeers
Consolidated Mines
Limited.) *B.* The cross
section shows a
reconstruction of the pipe
prior to erosion, the present
ground surface, and the
mined-out zone. (Diagram
after Arthur Holmes.)

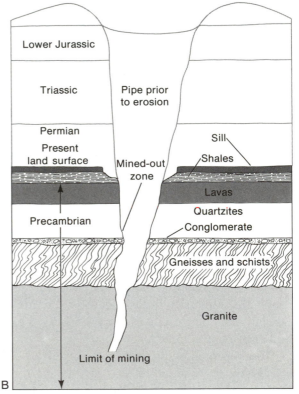

Lower Jurassic

Triassic

Pipe prior
to erosion

Permian

Sill

Present
land surface

Shales

Mined-out
zone

Lavas

Precambrian

Quartzites

Conglomerate

Gneisses and schists

Granite

Limit of mining

B

119 Ol Doinyo Lengai, Mountain of God, in Tanzania, East Africa. The high content of sodium carbonate in lavas from Ol Doinyo Lengai is unique, suggesting that it may be related to the type of volcanism which forms diamond pipes. (Photograph by Richard Stoiber.)

low temperatures — about half that of basaltic lava — apparently result from the high sodium carbonate content of the Ol Doinyo Lengai lavas. The soda acts as a flux, reducing melting temperature the same way it does in making commercial bottle glass.

Even if they are not emplacing diamonds, most of the world's active volcanoes are probably forming some type of hydrothermal deposits beneath their surface today. This is also true of geothermal reservoirs in which the circulating underground hot water is selectively dissolving, transporting, and depositing the more soluble minerals within the porous rocks. On a geologic time scale, today's volcanoes and geothermal systems are tomorrow's ore deposits.

The fact that a natural geothermal area like Yellowstone has a life span of ten thousand to hundreds of thousands of years indicates that volcanic ore deposits form quite slowly — drop by drop, atom by atom. People and their machines have voracious appetites for minerals, consuming them at rates far in excess of nature's patient creation. The message here is clear: we must recycle whatever mineral wealth we can or wait eons for new supplies.

14
Volcanoes and Climate

120 Vesuvius, 1944. (Photograph by the U.S. Navy, courtesy of the National Archives.)

209

In one period we believe ourselves governed
by immutable laws; in the next by chance.

—LOREN EISELEY (1907 – 1977)

. . . .

Bad weather has been blamed on almost everything from atomic bombs, sun spots, and the industrial revolution to volcanoes, black magic, the Republicans, and the Democrats. While most bad weather probably results from the natural variability of atmospheric processes, at least two of the above culprits — volcanoes and the industrial revolution — have put large amounts of debris and gas into the atmosphere, and thus appear more suspect than some of the others (Figure 120).

Benjamin Franklin was the first to suggest that volcanoes modify climate and weather. When Laki Volcano in Iceland erupted in 1783 with the largest effusion of lava in history, an enormous amount of gas was released (Figure 121). A blue haze or "dry fog" enveloped Iceland and much of northern Europe for months. The gas must have contained a significant amount of fluorine because livestock grazing on contaminated grass in Iceland died of fluoridosis. The widespread death of livestock — 11,000 cattle, 28,000 horses, and 190,000 sheep — resulted in a severe famine in which 10,000 Icelanders, one-fifth of the population, perished. The "dry fog" reaching Europe was more annoying than poisonous, but it was prevalent on many days during the summer and fall of 1783 and was apparently observed by Franklin during his stay in France. Since the winter of 1783 – 1784 was abnormally severe, especially in Europe, Franklin suggested that fine ash and gases from the Laki eruption may have

121 Cinder cones along the Laki fissure in Iceland. This fissure erupted in 1783 with the greatest lava flood in recorded history. The gases released during this enormous eruption caused a blue haze or "dry fog" that reached Europe.

filtered out enough of the sun's rays to cause the cold weather.

In 1815 Tambora Volcano shook the island of Sumbawa with a gigantic explosive eruption. Sumbawa is the second island east of Bali in Indonesia. Recent expeditions to Tambora estimate that the amount of magma expelled in high ash clouds and pyroclastic flows during that great eruption amounted to about 40 cubic kilometers. Although there is little data on the actual atmospheric effects from Tambora's huge explosion and caldera collapse, 1816 was remembered in Europe and America as the "year without a summer."

The idea that a volcanic eruption could have an effect on world climate surfaced again after the eruption of Krakatau in 1883. This time, the visible atmospheric effects were unquestionably worldwide; they began within two weeks of the great explosive eruption and lasted for months. Strange colors and halos of the sun and moon were noted, and there were vivid sunrises and sunsets for months on end (Figure 122). A Ceylon newspaper for September 17, 1883, gave this account:

> The sun for the last three days rises in a splendid green when he is visible; about 10° above the horizon. As he advances he assumes a beautiful blue, and as he comes further on looks a brilliant blue, resembling burning sulfur . . . even at the zenith, the light is blue, varying from pale blue to a light blue later on, somewhat similar to moonlight. . . . Then as he declines, the sun assumes the same changes, but vice versa.

Solar radiation decreased 10 percent over the next 3 years in Europe, and average world temperatures appeared to be below normal (Figure 123). At this point, however, the data become questionable. Most weather observations in the 1880s were made in Europe, and critics of the theory of volcanic influences on weather and climate point out that while Europe was colder, South America might have been

122 A. Approximate distribution of sky phenomena between August 26 and September 7, 1883. B. Approximate limits of the main sky phenomena at the end of November 1883. High-speed stratospheric winds averaging nearly 120 kilometers per hour carried the fine volcanic dust of the 1883 Krakatau eruption westward around the globe. By the end of November, the stratospheric haze covered over 70 percent of the Earth's surface causing spectacular sunsets and strange optical phenomena. (After C. J. Symons, ed., *The Eruption of Krakatoa.* Royal Society Report of the Krakatoa Committee, 1888.)

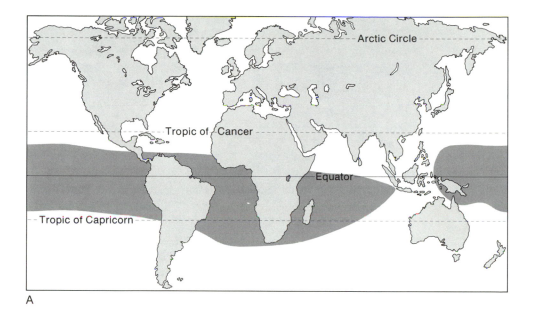

A

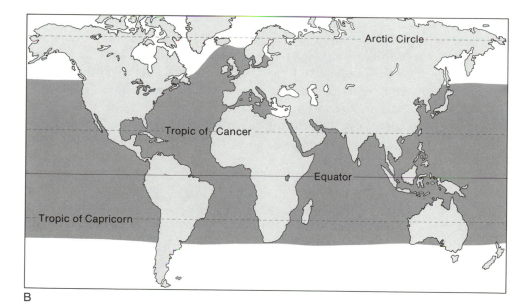

B

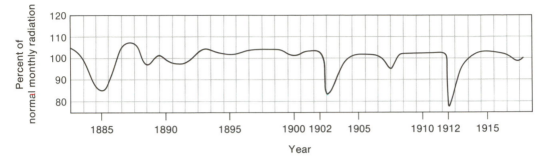

123 Average monthly intensity of solar radiation at the Earth's surface from 1883 to 1918 in relation to normal monthly values. Reductions of 10 to 20 percent occur after the eruptions of Krakatau in 1883; Pelée, Soufrière, and Santa Maria in 1902; and Katmai in 1912. (After Kimball, *Monthly Weather Review* 46, 1918, p. 355.)

warmer, and thus the true average world effects were not known.

Nevertheless, the theory has been tenacious. Harry Wexler, once Chief Scientist of the U.S. Weather Bureau, was a strong proponent of the idea. In 1952 he suggested that the warming trend of world temperatures since 1900 might be caused by the lack of major volcanic eruptions in the first half of the twentieth century. By contrast, he blamed the colder decades closing the nineteenth century on a series of major eruptions: Krakatau in 1883; Tarawera in New Zealand, 1886; Bandai-San in Japan, 1888; and Bogoslof in Alaska, 1890 (Figure 124).

H. H. Lamb, a British climatologist, has also been a champion of the concept that volcanic activity affects climate. He compiled a detailed list of volcanic eruptions since A.D. 1500 and computed a "dust veil index" based on the apparent amount of volcanic debris scattered into the atmosphere. He concluded that there has been a definite relationship between world climatic trends and large volcanic eruptions.

Recently, J. P. Kennett and R. C. Thunell, working with cores from deep-sea-drilling projects, concluded that the

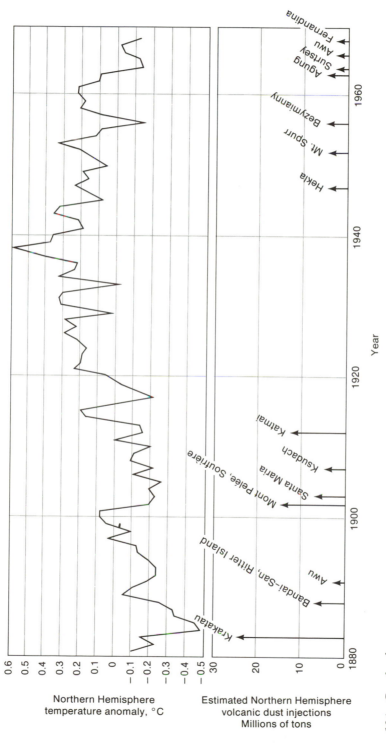

124 Graph of average temperature variations in the Northern Hemisphere and major volcanic eruptions that injected dust into the stratosphere. (After Robert Oliver, *Journal of Applied Meteorology* 15, 1976, p. 934.)

amount of volcanic ash in seafloor sediments increased about 2 million years ago and has stayed high since then. The period of the last 2 million years coincides with the Pleistocene ice ages, and Kennett and Thunell conclude that the extra volcanism and extra cold are not just a coincidence. But even this evidence is not conclusive; some scientists point out that not enough sea cores of the older sediments have yet been taken to make a valid comparison.

If volcanic gas and dust do alter weather and climate, the effect probably operates in the stratosphere (above 10 kilometers) where the layer of haze hovers for a long time because there are no clouds and rain to wash it away quickly (Figure 125). Meteorologists have identified a long-lasting

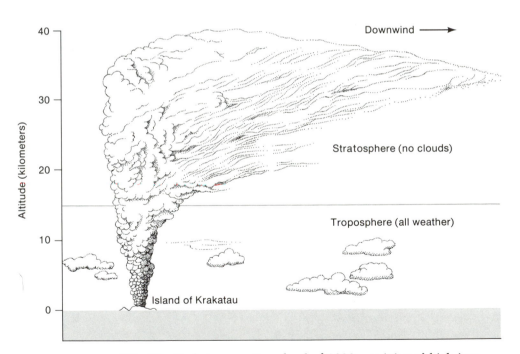

125 The Krakatau eruption cloud of 1883 was injected high into the stratosphere, where no rain clouds exist to wash the debris back to Earth. Once there, the fine dust stays in suspension for months to years. (After Richard Hazlett, 1978.)

stratospheric aerosol layer at heights of 15 to 30 kilometers that seems to be composed of a thin haze of small particles or droplets, smaller than .001 millimeter in diameter. These particles are made up of various materials including sea salt, silicate dust, and sulfuric acid. They probably originate from several sources — sea spray, dust storms, volcanic eruptions, forest fires, industrial smokestacks, and so on. The density of the aerosol layer changes over periods of months to years. It can increase suddenly with an injection of new aerosol from a volcanic eruption, but it takes several years to decrease to normal.

This layer of haze in the stratosphere apparently intercepts the incoming sunlight, heating the stratosphere and cooling the lower atmosphere as well as the Earth's surface. The 1963 eruption of Mount Agung volcano in Bali, Indonesia, provided some of the first measurable evidence that this effect is real. The Balinese consider Agung to be the navel of the world, and they live with respect and reverence for this 3142-meter stratovolcano. After 120 years of repose Mount Agung began erupting on February 18, 1963. Major explosions produced destructive glowing avalanches on March 17 and May 16 that devastated many villages and killed 2000 people.

The explosion clouds of gas and volcanic dust reached heights of more than 10 kilometers above the crater, apparently high enough to inject volcanic debris into the stratosphere. The atmospheric effects, including fiery red sunsets and halos around the sun and moon, encircled the Earth within a few weeks; but the most convincing evidence was the decrease in starlight measured worldwide by astronomical observatories; the decrease was maximum from August to November 1963 and lasted until mid-1964. Measured stratospheric temperatures rose as much as 6°C, and the average world temperature dropped 0.4°C for 3 years after the eruption.

Although Agung was a major eruption, the explosion of Krakatau in 1883 was at least 10 times greater, both in terms of energy and the total volume of volcanic products. The key question, however, is how much volcanic dust and gas reached into the stratosphere from Agung as compared to Krakatau, and that is not known.

When Mount St. Helens erupted violently in 1980 the ash cloud during the first half hour of intense activity was propelled higher than 24 kilometers. For the next 8 hours, radar tracking of the top of the erupting cloud indicated an average altitude of only 16 kilometers. The amount of ash hurled into the sky was estimated to be 500 million tons, much of it in particles about 1/10 millimeter in diameter. The high-altitude cloud moved eastward across the United States in 3 days, with most ash falling out within 400 kilometers, but with a light dusting as far east as Denver, Colorado.

Despite the magnitude of the Mount St. Helens eruption, there were little or no apparent worldwide atmospheric or surface-cooling effects. Although similar in many ways to the eruption of Agung, Mount St. Helens' injection of volcanic ash into the stratosphere did not have the same effect on world climate. Why was there such a difference? Was it the size of ash particles? The latitude of the volcano? Some unknown difference in gas content? Perhaps all these factors were involved.

Details are scarce about the size of the Agung cloud, just how high it went, and how fine the ash particles were, but Agung is close to the equator so its stratospheric dust and gas cloud could circulate over both hemispheres of the Earth. The Mount St. Helens cloud, however, was injected at 46° North Latitude, and its effects were limited to the Northern Hemisphere. After the first half hour of the St. Helens eruption the cloud was barely reaching the lower stratosphere, and most of the ash particles were large enough to fall from the cloud within hours.

The volcanic gas that lofted the Mount St. Helens cloud was mainly steam and carbon dioxide, with small amounts of sulfur gases. Two years later a Mexican volcano showed that stratospheric volcanic clouds with high sulfur dioxide content have a much more profound atmospheric effect.

El Chichón Volcano in southern Mexico, dormant since prehistoric times and thought to be extinct, blasted into action in late March 1982. In one climactic week three major explosions lofted large ash and gas clouds to heights of 20 to 25 kilometers. Two to three thousand people in villages near El Chichón were killed by pyroclastic flows that accompanied the eruption.

The Mount St. Helens eruption was larger in terms of volume of rock involved, but El Chichón's atmospheric effects were far greater. Besides fine ash particles, El Chichón injected an enormous amount of sulfur dioxide into the stratosphere. This gas soon oxidized, picked up water vapor, and formed tiny droplets of sulfuric acid. The acid aerosol and fine ash were carried westward by high-speed stratospheric winds, circling the Earth within a month.

Measured by LIDAR in Hawaii, the El Chichón stratospheric haze was more than 100 times more opaque than the Mount St. Helens cloud had been. LIDAR is a technique of aiming a laser beam into the clear sky and measuring the backscatter of laser light that is reflected from fine particles or aerosol droplets suspended in the atmosphere. It took nearly a year for the El Chichón stratospheric cloud to attain its maximum effect over Europe, and it was not until 1985 that LIDAR measurements returned to levels seen before the eruption (Figure 126).

The effect of El Chichón's eruption on global weather has been a subject of debate. In 1982–1983 a major disturbance in the ocean and atmospheric currents occurred in the equatorial Pacific. A similar pattern occurs occasionally, and is called El Niño. Drought in Australia and heavy rains in California, as well as other unusual weather in 1982–1983, were attributed to El Niño. Could the El Chichón cloud have triggered this disturbance? Some meteorologists speculated that there may have been a connection; others considered the sequence a coincidence. No significant global cooling of the Earth followed the El Chichón eruption, but there is no question that the aerosol formed a thick haze layer in the stratosphere over the Northern Hemisphere until 1985.

The Earth has actually been in a warming trend the last few years. Some meteorologists blame this on increasing carbon dioxide in the atmosphere, caused by burning of fossil

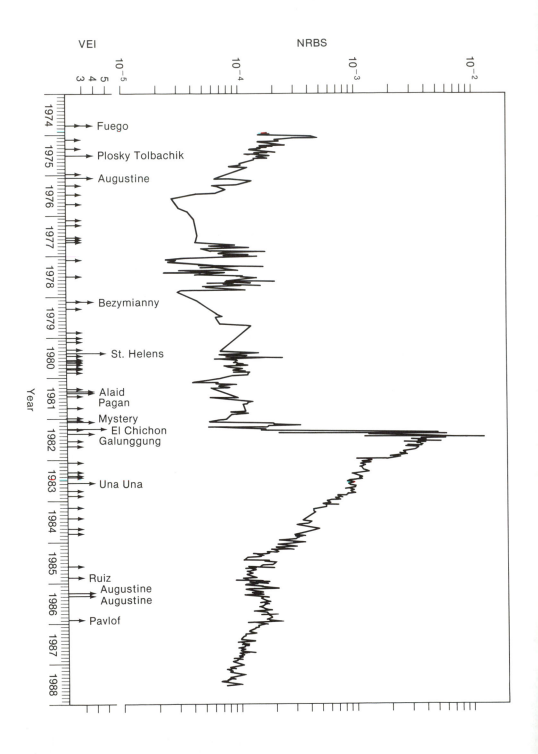

fuels and by the destruction of rain forests that consume carbon dioxide. Carbon dioxide in the atmosphere has a "greenhouse effect." It is transparent to light but more opaque to infrared radiation; warming of the Earth by sunlight during the day is not affected, but cooling of the Earth at night by infrared radiation into space is retarded. The carbon dioxide acts like the windows in a greenhouse; light comes in but heat can't escape. The net effect is a global warming of the Earth's surface. In the absence of this warming greenhouse effect, the cooling influence of El Chichón's volcanic cloud might have been much more pronounced.

The question remains: To what extent do volcanic eruptions affect our weather and climate? Evidence seems to show that eruptions injecting large amounts of fine ash and, even more importantly, great quantities of sulfur dioxide gas into the stratosphere do significantly affect the solar radiation reaching the Earth's surface. Major explosive eruptions, particularly in equatorial regions where their ash and gas clouds may affect both hemispheres, seem to be capable of lowering average global temperature by as much as 1°C. An extremely large event like the Yellowstone eruption 600,000 years ago, or a series of major explosive eruptions that prolong the stratospheric haze layer for decades or centuries, would probably have a much greater cooling effect.

126 Integrated backscatter coefficient obtained by LIDAR at Mauna Loa Observatory, Hawaii. Total backscatter plotted is from an altitude of from 16 to 33 kilometers. The effect of the El Chichón cloud is nearly 100 times greater than stratospheric haze from other explosive eruptions measured since 1974. Moderate to large volcanic explosions are shown by arrows along the base of the graph. VEI (volcanic explosivity index) magnitudes are logarithmic. For example, the 1980 eruption of Mount St. Helens (VEI = 5) was 10 times larger than the 1983 eruption of Una Una. (From Thomas DeFoor and Elmer Robinson, Mauna Loa Observatory, NOAA-ERL, 1988.)

However, volcanic eruptions are only one factor among many that affect weather and climate. The normal interaction of the atmosphere, oceans, and land surface is extremely complex. Add to this the disruption by both man-made and natural causes, and the intricacy of the problem begins to be seen. It is a joint task for geologists, meteorologists, and climatologists to understand and quantify these effects. Such understanding is of immense importance to a world that depends on a benign climate for its very existence.

15

Forecasting Volcanic Eruptions

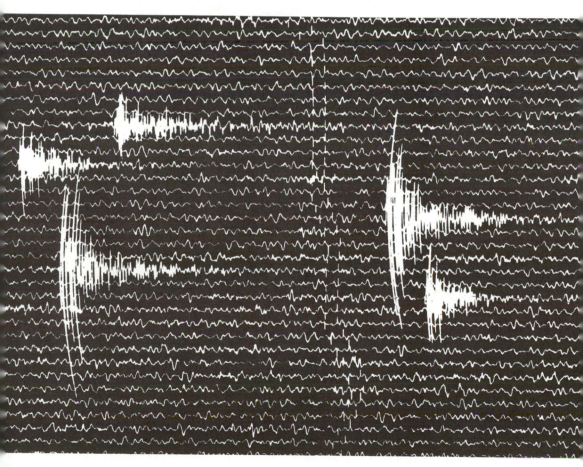

127 Seismogram of small earthquakes related to volcanic activity in Hawaii.
(Photograph by the U.S. Geological Survey.)

Nature cannot be commanded except by being obeyed.
—Sir Francis Bacon (1561–1626)

. . . .

Forecasting the time, place, and character of volcanic eruptions is one of the major goals in volcanology. We prefer the word *forecast* to *prediction* because the science of weather forecasting has established the concept that forecasts are probabilistic. That is, they are not precise; the hope is that they are more accurate than statistical averages.

For example, suppose that rainfall records in Hilo, Hawaii, show that on the average it rains during 6 out of 10 days throughout the year. If a weatherman forecasts a 60 percent chance of rain tomorrow in Hilo he is not making a very adventurous statement. However, if the wind patterns and satellite photos indicate that chances are greater or less than average for rain tomorrow, then the forecast may say 90 percent chance of rain, or 10 percent chance of rain.

These would be valid forecasts based on information other than historical statistics; their worth can be evaluated in hindsight by comparison to random guesses. Weather forecasters avoid the word *prediction* because it sounds so precise and specific. Present weather forecasts, although far from exact, are extremely valuable. They do much better than random guesses, and their batting average is improving.

The current goal in forecasting volcanic eruptions is to provide the best forecasts possible based on the geologic history of the volcano under study as well as on the day-to-day vital signs of the volcano in terms of earthquakes, surface deformation, temperature, gas emissions, and other measurements.

The statistics of past eruptions are of great importance both as a basis for finding the average probability of eruption and as a means of deciphering some pattern in eruption habits. At least three patterns can be recognized even though the period of repose between eruptions varies from days to thousands of years.

One pattern is completely random. That is, no matter how long the repose period has been, the average chance for an eruption next month remains the same. This is like cutting cards to get an ace; no matter how many times you fail, the chance in the next cut is exactly the same: 4 out of 52. Mauna Loa Volcano in Hawaii appears to operate in this random manner; no matter how long or short the repose between eruptions, the average chance for a new eruption next month remains the same — 2 percent.

Hekla Volcano in Iceland shows quite a different pattern of time intervals between eruptions. At Hekla the average probability of an eruption increases with time. This would be like cutting for aces and discarding the cut card each time you fail, thereby increasing the chance of getting an ace with each new cut.

Just the opposite occurs at volcanoes like Kilauea in Hawaii, where a group of eruptions will cluster together in time (Figure 128). In this situation the probability of an eruption decreases with time. There is no easy analogy for this in card-cutting.

Each of these time patterns in eruptive habit is important as a basis for forecasting future activity. Unfortunately, for the statistics to have any meaning, the number of eruptions must exceed 10 or 20. Only a small fraction of the world's volcanoes are active enough or have been studied long enough to establish these patterns.

Dormant volcanoes are by no means dead, and by studying them with sensitive instruments it is possible to monitor their vital signs through periods of repose and awakening. The earthquake count is one of these vital signs.

Earthquakes and volcanoes both occur along plate margins, where most of the earthquakes are considered to be related to the slow grinding of the moving edges of the plates.

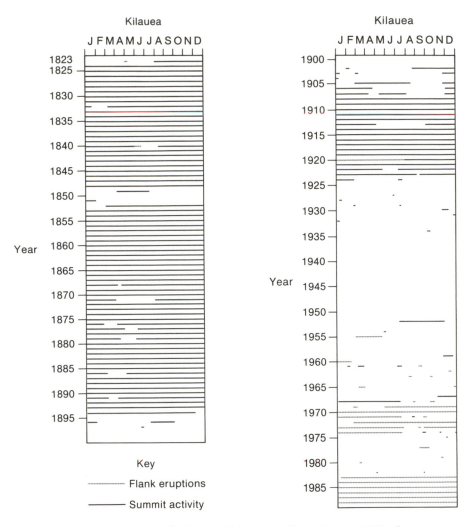

128 Eruptions of Kilauea Volcano in Hawaii since 1823 show a
pattern of long periods of continuing eruptions or groups of
eruptions interspersed with long periods of repose. The periods from
1823 to 1894 and from 1906 to 1924 were characterized by nearly
continuous lava lake activity in the summit crater. (After Gordon
Macdonald and Douglass Hubbard, *Volcanoes of the National Parks
of Hawaii*, Hawaii Natural History Association, 1982.)

However, some earthquakes appear to be more directly related to volcanic processes. In Hawaii and other areas of hot-spot volcanoes, earthquakes accompany volcanism even though the plate margins may be thousands of miles away (Figures 127 and 129). In fact, Hawaii's Kilauea Volcano is one of the most seismically active areas on Earth. Ten or more microearthquakes occur beneath the volcano on an average day, and an earthquake large enough to be felt occurs about once a week.

During the immediate prelude to an eruption as new magma conduits are opening underground, hundreds to thousands of microearthquakes shake the seismometers, with several felt shocks generally accompanying these earthquake swarms. At volcanoes like Mount St. Helens that are related to subduction zones, the number of microearthquakes during dormant periods is usually only a few per month, but the swarms preceding an eruption generally increase the count of small quakes to several hundred per day.

There is probably more than one cause for these volcanic earthquakes, including increasing topographic load, underground temperature changes, moving magma, and gas explosions. The slipping and cracking of rocks underground to adjust to the growing weight of a huge volcano is only indirectly related to volcanic activity, but the other causes, particularly the movement of magma and the formation of cracks through which it can move, are closely connected to active volcanic processes.

Increases in the number or size of volcanic earthquakes, particularly those related to the conduits through which magma erupts to the surface, usually occur before eruptions. However, the relationship is not infallible. In a study of 71 earthquake swarms and volcanic eruptions, 58 percent showed an increase in earthquake activity before eruptions, 38 percent showed an increase without eruptions, and in 4 percent there was an eruption without any apparent increase in earthquake activity.

Because the background count of microearthquakes in volcanic areas is highly variable, only a large change in their

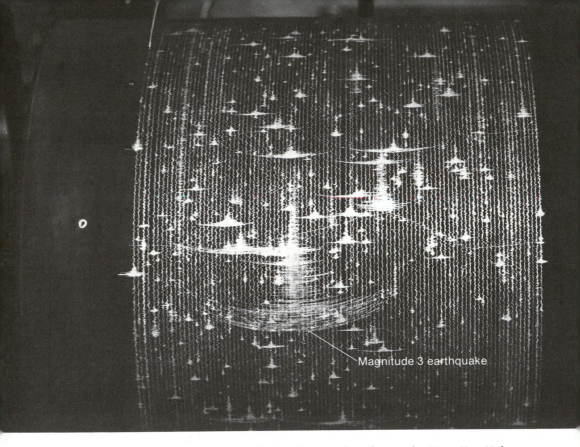

Magnitude 3 earthquake

129 Seismograph recording earthquakes at the Hawaiian Volcano Observatory. The drum rotates once every 15 minutes, slowly enough that an entire day fits on one record sheet. Most of the microearthquakes on this record are too small to be felt. However, the larger quake, whose seismogram is just to the left and below center, is about magnitude 3, large enough to be felt in a local area close to its source. (Photograph by the U.S. Geological Survey.)

number, by as much as a factor of 100, seems to be significant. Soviet scientists in Kamchatka now think that large increases in the total energy released by volcanic earthquakes is more important than their increasing number. The time between the onset of increasing earthquakes and the actual eruption varies from months to hours, but even so, the number, size, and location of earthquakes on active volcanoes is an important index to their forthcoming activity.

Volcanic tremor is a unique kind of seismic activity associated with volcanoes. It consists of more-or-less continuous ground vibration with a frequency of 0.5 to 10 cycles per second—a very low hum detectable by seismographs (Figure 130). Its source is not clear; various studies relate it to the formation of gas bubbles or the turbulent flow of magma, which creates a resonance like water hammering in poorly designed pipes. Whatever its source, it is nearly always present during a volcanic eruption, and often begins before the actual surface outbreak. However, not all periods of volcanic tremor are followed by an eruption. In Hawaii, high-amplitude volcanic tremor is often the best indication that an

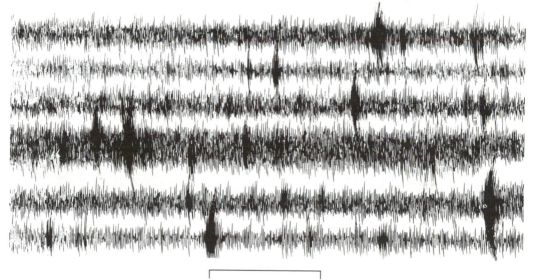

1 minute

130 Volcanic tremor recorded on a seismograph in Hawaii during the eruption of Kilauea in 1977. This low-frequency vibration of the ground at about 3 to 5 cycles per second is related to the movement of magma through underground conduits. The tremor starts before the breakout of eruptions and is a sign that an eruption is likely to occur. (Photograph by James Griggs, U.S. Geological Survey.)

eruption has begun or is about to begin within a few minutes or hours. A "tremor alarm" ringing in the houses of the Observatory staff brings them running regardless of the time of night.

Slight changes in the slopes or distances between survey points on the summits and flanks of active volcanoes provide another major method of diagnosing the internal changes taking place. Several techniques are involved, including conventional leveling and the determination of distances with reflected laser beams. Tiltmeters, which can detect changes in slope smaller than 1 part per million, are also used. An angular change in slope of 1 part per million (1 microradian) is equivalent to lifting the end of a rigid board 1 kilometer long by only 1 millimeter. A promising new technique called GPS (Global Positioning System) uses satellites and portable receivers to determine the relative position of the ground stations to accuracies of a few millimeters (Figure 131). Radio code and time signals broadcast by the satellites arrive at ground-surface survey stations in a unique pattern. Comparison by computer processing of the different patterns recorded at two survey stations determines their relative location.

Both elevation and distance changes are detectable by GPS measurements; the receivers can be many kilometers apart, and need to "see" the satellites but not each other. Although the present instruments and data-reduction computers are quite expensive, important observations can be made in a few hours with only one person at each receiver.

Repeated at frequent intervals, these surveying techniques reveal the tiny, unseeable deformations of the volcano's surface caused by changes in magmatic pressure or volume inside the volcano. *Deformation monitoring*, the collective name for all of these surveying techniques, has become the second most important means of forecasting volcanic eruptions, preceded only by the monitoring of earthquakes.

The slow inflation of Kilauea Volcano in the months before an eruption, and the sudden collapse over a period of hours or days during an eruption (described in Chapter 6),

131 GPS (Global Positioning System) antenna is set up over a survey benchmark and receives radio time and code signals from passing satellites. Elevations and distances between two or more receivers operating simultaneously can be determined to accuracies of better than one part per million.

has been revealed by deformation measurements in the past 30 years (Figure 132). The slow, more-or-less continuous addition of magma into the shallow chamber beneath Kilauea's summit causes the summit to swell upward as much

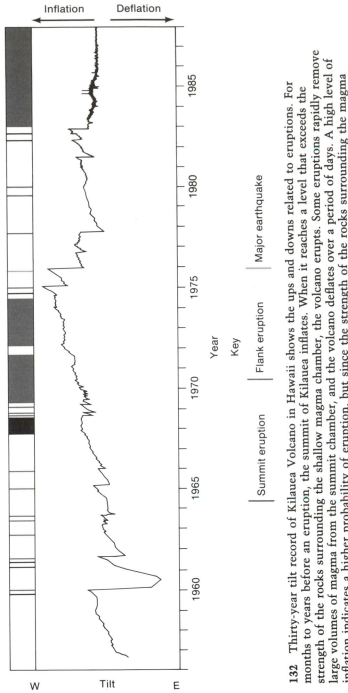

132 Thirty-year tilt record of Kilauea Volcano in Hawaii shows the ups and downs related to eruptions. For months to years before an eruption, the summit of Kilauea inflates. When it reaches a level that exceeds the strength of the rocks surrounding the shallow magma chamber, the volcano erupts. Some eruptions rapidly remove large volumes of magma from the summit chamber, and the volcano deflates over a period of days. A high level of inflation indicates a higher probability of eruption, but since the strength of the rocks surrounding the magma chamber varies from one eruption to another, no exact level of tilt can be used to predict the next eruption. (Data from the U.S. Geological Survey.)

as 2 meters over a diameter of 10 kilometers. This gentle bulge causes outward tilts and increasing distances between survey stations, similar to the changing relationship of spots on the surface of an inflating balloon.

Most eruptions of Kilauea remove molten lava from the magma chamber faster than it is replenished, causing summit deflation, inward tilts, and contracting distances between survey stations. Deformation measurements provide a kind of magma barometer that in turn can be used to help forecast eruptions. If there were an exact level of inflation that triggered an eruption, the question of when an eruption will occur would be solved.

But nature is not that simple. On Kilauea, which has been tracked through more deformation cycles than any other single volcano, the degree of tilt at the Volcano Observatory just prior to eruptions has always been relatively high, but has not shown any specific critical angle. The reason for this may be that an increase in either pressure or volume in the shallow magma chamber beneath Kilauea can cause uplift and outward tilt of the summit area. Increases in volume that occur slowly may not cause equal increases in pressure, and it is increasing pressure that causes the hard rocks surrounding the magma chamber to split apart. Magma moves into these newly formed underground cracks and the summit subsides rapidly. The magma may halt underground in these new fractures as a shallow intrusion, or it may break to the surface in an eruption.

Deformation measurements on several potentially explosive volcanoes of subducting plate margins are now under way, but it is not yet clear whether they will be as useful as those on basaltic shield volcanoes. One problem with explosive volcanoes is their long repose time between eruptions. It could take several hundred years to learn as much about the deformation at Vesuvius as has already been learned at Kilauea in the last 30 years. Nevertheless, monitoring both the earthquake swarm and large surface bulge that occurred for nearly 2 months before the major eruption of Mount St. Helens in 1980 provided important insights into understand-

ing what was going on beneath the volcano during that period (see Chapter 4).

Changes in the Earth's magnetic and electrical fields near
volcanoes, which relate to the state of volcanic activity, have
been observed in Japan, New Zealand, Kamchatka, and Hawaii. Although the techniques used for these observations are
relatively new and not as well established as seismic and
deformation measurements, their usefulness looks promising.

Temperature changes at steam vents and warm springs on
volcanoes would seem to be an obvious index for forecasting,
but rainfall and changes in groundwater circulation often
cause large fluctuations in temperature not related to volcanic activity. In one case, however, the 12°C temperature
rise of the crater lake at Taal Volcano in the Philippines
clearly signaled its 1965 eruption (Figure 133).

Geochemical changes in the volume and composition of
volcanic gases are also useful indicators of hidden changes
beneath active volcanoes. New steam vents formed at Askja
Volcano in Iceland two weeks before its 1961 eruption. Scientists in Japan, Kamchatka, and the United States have all
reported an increase in sulfur gases relative to chloride gases
at volcanic steam vents in the years or days before some
eruptions. Changes in the percentage of hydrogen, helium,
and radon in volcanic gases are also under study as possible
signals of changing volcanic activity.

No single technique appears to be the master key to forecasting volcanic eruptions. Each volcano is unique, and the
case history of one cannot always be used to diagnose the
symptoms of another. Even so, useful though not precise
forecasting is currently being practiced on a few volcanoes in
Japan, Indonesia, Iceland, the Philippines, Kamchatka, and
Hawaii. Some recent notable successes and failures illustrate
the present state of the art.

Mauna Loa Volcano in Hawaii erupted on July 5 and 6,
1975, after 25 years of repose, its longest sleep since records
began in the mid-nineteenth century. Thirty million cubic

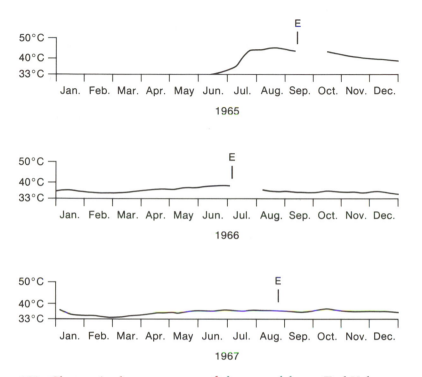

133 Changes in the temperature of the crater lake on Taal Volcano in the Philippines sometimes warn of forthcoming eruptions. In 1965 the temperature began to rise well above its background level of 33°C in July; the volcano erupted in September. The 1966 eruption was preceded by a much less obvious temperature rise, and the 1967 eruption could not have been forecast on the basis of temperature alone. (Data from A. Alcaraz, Philippine Commission on Volcanology.)

meters of lava poured out in that brief but intense summit eruption. Earthquake and deformation monitoring of Mauna Loa was increased during and after the eruption, and scientists waited with interest to find what these observations would reveal while Mauna Loa rested and prepared itself for the next eruption. It was a 10-year wait; Figure 134 sums up the data.

Small earthquakes of shallow and intermediate depth had shown an increase for 1 to 2 years before both the 1975 and 1984 eruptions, but the number of earthquakes deeper than 13 kilometers showed no change. The sharp increase in intermediate-depth earthquakes in late 1983 was caused by numerous aftershocks that followed a magnitude 6.6 earthquake beneath the east flank of Mauna Loa in November of that year.

Deformation measurements of the summit showed a 75-millimeter increase in the length of a 3-kilometer-long survey line across the caldera in the year before the 1975 eruption, and a similar increase prior to the 1984 activity. At the onset of both eruptions the summit caldera widened suddenly by about ½ meter. This was caused by the opening of the magma-filled cracks that split the caldera and fed the eruptions.

Following the start of the eruption in 1984 the caldera width contracted by 300 millimeters; this occurred because the Northeast Rift Zone vents at 2900 meters drained part of the summit magma reservoir and caused the summit to subside and contract. After the 3-week-long 1984 eruption of 220 million cubic meters of lava (Figure 135), the summit began to reinflate and widen again. By 1988 the summit inflation and stretching had recovered about 50 percent of the subsidence and contraction that accompanied the flank eruption.

Because of the increase in earthquakes and summit inflation, an eruption forecast had been published in 1983 indicating a significant increase in the probability of Mauna Loa

134 Earthquakes and deformation are precursors to eruptions of Mauna Loa in Hawaii. Shallow and intermediate-depth quakes beneath the volcano, most of them too small to be felt, increase for 1 to 2 years before an eruption. Widening of the 3-kilometer-wide caldera (each dot is a separate survey) occurs mainly during eruptions. (After J. P. Lockwood and others, U.S. Geological Survey Professional Paper 1350, 1987, pp. 548–49.)

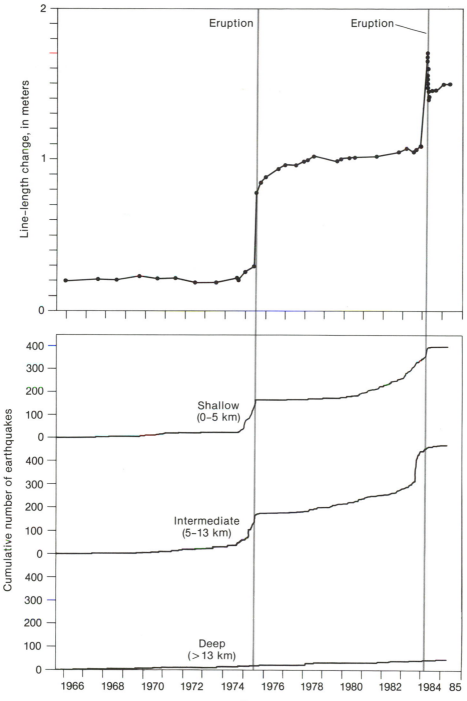

Eruption

Eruption

Line-length change, in meters

2

1

0

Cumulative number of earthquakes

400
300
200
100
0

Shallow
(0–5 km)

400
300
200
100
0

Intermediate
(5–13 km)

400
300
200
100
0

Deep
(>13 km)

1966 1968 1970 1972 1974 1976 1978 1980 1982 1984 85

Year

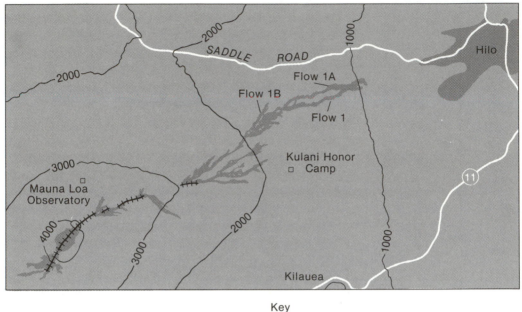

Key

0   5   10 km

Contour interval 1000 meters   +++++++++ Eruptive vents

Lava flows

135 Fissure vents and lava flows of the 1984 Mauna Loa eruption. After the initial outbreak at the summit, eruptive fissures opened progressively down the northeast rift. The fractures at the 2900-meter elevation opened 15 hours after the eruption began and remained the principal vents of the 3-week-long eruption. Flow 1 reached its maximum length in 5 days and then diverted itself upstream into flow 1A. Flow 1B formed by similar channel clogging of flow 1A on April 5, and Hilo was no longer threatened by the eruption. (After J. P. Lockwood and others, U.S. Geological Survey Professional Paper 1350, 1987, p. 561.)

erupting during the next 2 years. The precursors for the 1984 eruption were of two time scales: those that began about a year before, and those that preceded the outbreak by only 2 hours. An earthquake swarm and tremor were picked up on the Mauna Loa seismometers at 11:30 P.M. on March 24 and the eruption began at 1:25 A.M. on March 25. Some precursors a few days or weeks before a Mauna Loa eruption would be most useful to discover.

The Soviets may be doing better. The huge eruption of Tolbachik Volcano in Kamchatka in 1975 was preceded by a major earthquake swarm. Volcanologist P. I. Tokarev's published forecast that an eruption was imminent in the Tolbachik region during the next week allowed Russian television crews to be on hand for the birth of a new volcano on July 6, just 2 days after the forecast was issued (Figure 136).

However, real danger from volcanic hazards remains both a threat and a predicament to society. In 1976 a small eruption of La Soufrière on Guadeloupe led to the massive and expensive evacuation of 70,000 residents because of the threat that the eruption might climax in catastrophic nuées ardentes similar to those of the Mont Pelée eruption on the neighboring island of Martinique in 1902. Fortunately, no major eruption took place; but unfortunately, volcanologists were blamed for their "cry wolf" forecast.

The eruptions of Mount St. Helens (described in Chapter 4) illustrate both the present strengths and weaknesses of volcano forecasting. Based on that volcano's geologic history, a warning was published in 1978 that destructive eruptions might occur within a few decades. After small eruptions began in March 1980, the strong, ongoing earthquake swarm and fast-growing bulge indicated to geologists monitoring Mount St. Helens that a sizable shallow intrusion of magma was being injected beneath the north flank of the mountain.

The probability that the magma would reach the surface in a significant eruption was considered quite high. However, the timing and scale of the great May 18 eruption were not anticipated; even in reviewing the events in hindsight no specific precursors or precedents were detected that might have called for a complete evacuation of the area that was later devastated. Nevertheless, since the danger caused by the shallow intrusion of magma was recognized, access to the area was severely restricted and many hundreds of lives were saved.

136 Great Tolbachik eruption in Kamchatka in 1975 was accurately forecast on the basis of increasing local earthquakes. The total volume of lava and pyroclastics erupted was nearly 2 cubic kilometers, and the ash cloud reached 14 kilometers high. (Photograph by N. P. Smelov, Institute of Volcanology, Kamchatka, U.S.S.R.)

Following the great eruption, five smaller explosions occurred during 1980, and the lava dome in the crater has grown rapidly during several periods between 1980 and 1987. Beginning with the July 1980 explosion, all the eruptions and dome-building events at Mount St. Helens have been accurately forecast from increases in seismicity and rates of deformation. These precursors, which have occurred days to hours before each eruptive event, have given sufficient warning to allow evacuation of the hazardous areas.

But the lessons learned at Mount St. Helens do not always apply to other volcanoes. Rabaul, in Papua New Guinea, is a port city built in the ocean-breached ruins of a prehistoric caldera. Volcanoes nearby are still active, and an eruption in 1937 killed 500 people in Rabaul.

In 1983 a major earthquake swarm and uplift in the area were detected by the Rabaul Volcano Observatory (Figure 137). During 1983–1984, 92,000 shallow earthquakes were recorded, many felt by the 70,000 residents who live on the rim of the great harbor. The measured uplift that accompanied the earthquake swarm was 63 centimeters, but maximum uplift beneath the sea was probably more than that.

Scientists at the Rabaul Volcano Observatory concluded that a significant intrusion of magma was being injected at a depth of about 2 kilometers beneath the caldera, and plans were made to evacuate the city. But in late 1984 the earthquake swarm and uplift waned and the region has been stable through 1988.

Apparently the magma pressure was not high enough to force it to the surface, and as the intrusion from depth stopped, the crisis was over. Alarms of this type are not false alarms or crying wolf; the probability of an eruption was high during the seismic and deformation activity. "Aborted alarm" would be a better term. The wolf was there; fortunately he wasn't hungry.

The people living in Armero at the foot of Colombia's Nevado del Ruiz Volcano in 1985 were much less fortunate (see page 84). Earthquakes had been increasing beneath the

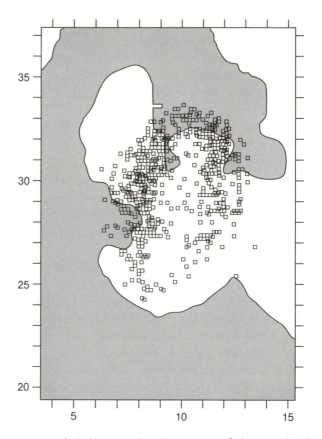

137 Locations of shallow earthquakes, most of them at depths of 3 kilometers or less, beneath Rabaul Caldera in Papua New Guinea, from September 1983 to November 1984. The area of maximum uplift was within the oval of earthquakes. Numbers along the axes indicate distance in kilometers. (From C. O. McKee and others, *Volcano News*, 1985, v. 19–20, p. 3.)

volcano for months and a small steam explosion burst out of the summit crater in September 1985. Because of the ice cap on the high summit and a record of 1000 people near Ruiz killed by mudflows in 1845, geologists warned the people living along the rivers draining the mountain that any eruption of molten or hot fragmental rock onto the summit ice could bring disaster.

Although warned, no one in Armero really knew what a mudflow was; when an eruption occurred in November only a few people evacuated the town. Two hours after a hot pyroclastic flow melted part of the ice cap, Armero was swept away by torrents of mud.

In hindsight, mudflow-detection devices or sentries upstream could have saved 22,000 lives. Forecasting an eruption is only one step toward reducing volcanic risk; contingency plans and actions are also essential.

Most infamous volcanoes owe their notoriety to the deaths and destruction they have caused. Eruptions where successful forecasts have saved thousands of lives are less well known. One such example occurred in Indonesia in 1983.

Colo Volcano, on the island of Una Una, was shaken by an earthquake swarm that began on July 14, and minor explosive eruptions began on July 18. On the basis of the past behavior of Colo and similar volcanoes, geologists from the Volcanological Survey of Indonesia recommended to the local governmental officials that the island be evacuated. The officials concurred, and all 7000 inhabitants were removed by boat.

The climax eruption on July 23 swept the island with hot pyroclastic flows. Most of the livestock and coconut plantations were destroyed. It will take years to rebuild the island's economy, but the people survived.

Few of the world's active volcanoes have been carefully studied and most are not being monitored. The methods and techniques to do this are fairly well established, but other, more immediate problems and dangers compete for the human and financial resources needed to carry out these investigations.

The study of volcanoes is a fledgling science. It has come a long way, but it has an even longer way to go on the path to a true understanding of volcanoes. This book is dedicated to those who will seek that path.

Glossary

. . . .

aa   A type of lava flow having a rough, fragmental surface.

active volcano   A volcano that is erupting or has erupted in recorded history.

airfall deposit   Pyroclastic fragments that have fallen from an eruption cloud.

andesite   A volcanic rock type intermediate in composition between dacite and basalt.

angle of repose   The steepest slope at which loose material will come to rest without slumping.

ash, volcanic   Fine pyroclastic material, down to dust size, that is formed by explosive volcanic eruptions.

barograph   An instrument that makes a continuous record of changes in atmospheric pressure.

basalt   A dark, heavy lava composed of about 50 percent silica, 15 percent alumina, and significant amounts of iron, calcium, and magnesium.

block, volcanic   A solid fragment thrown out in an explosive eruption, ranging in size from about 6 centimeters to several meters in diameter.

bomb, volcanic   A still-viscous lava lump thrown out in an explosive eruption, which takes on its rounded shape while in flight.

caldera   A gigantic basin with steep walls at the summit of a volcano; larger than a crater, and usually formed by collapse.

245

cinder cone   A steep conical hill formed by the accumulation of cinders and other loose material expelled from a volcanic vent by escaping gases.

cinder, volcanic   A pyroclastic fragment about 1 centimeter in diameter.

composite cone   See *stratovolcano*.

compressional margin   The converging edges of two tectonic plates.

conduit   The pipe or crack through which magma moves.

continental crust   The solid outer layers of the Earth including granitic rocks of the continent.

continental drift   The theory that horizontal movements of the Earth's surface cause slow relative movements of continents toward or away from one another.

crater   A bowl- or funnel-shaped depression, generally in the top of a volcanic cone; often the major vent of volcanic products.

crystalline rock   A hard rock composed of interlocking crystals; often of igneous origin.

dacite   A volcanic rock type intermediate in composition between rhyolite and andesite.

debris avalanche   Flowing or sliding, wet or dry mixture of soil and rock debris that moves at high speed.

dike   A sheetlike body of intrusive igneous rock that cuts across the layering of the host rock.

dormant volcano   A volcano that is not presently erupting but is considered likely to do so in the future.

dust, volcanic   The finer particles of volcanic ash.

earthquake swarm   A sequence of closely spaced earthquakes during which the energy release is approximately constant (as opposed to a sequence consisting of a large quake followed by diminishing aftershocks).

earthquake wave   A general term for a vibrational wave produced by an earthquake.

effusive eruption   An eruption consisting mainly of lava flows (as opposed to explosive eruption).

eruption cloud   A gaseous cloud of volcanic ash and other pyroclastics that forms by volcanic explosion.

extensional margin   The edges of tectonic plates that are moving apart.

extinct volcano   A volcano that is not erupting and is not expected to do so in the future; a dead volcano.

fault A fracture in the Earth's crust along which there has been movement.

feldspar A light-colored mineral composed largely of silicon, oxygen, and aluminum.

flank eruption Eruption from the side of a volcano (in contrast to a summit eruption).

fume A gaseous cloud without volcanic ash.

gabbro A coarse-grained igneous rock of basaltic composition.

geophysics The physical and mechanical aspects of geology (in contrast to geochemistry).

geothermal energy Energy derived from the internal heat of the Earth.

geothermal power Power generated by using the heat energy of the Earth.

granite A coarse-grained igneous rock composed mostly of quartz and feldspar.

heat transfer Movement of heat from one place to another.

hot-spot volcanoes Volcanoes related to a persistent heat source in the mantle.

hydrothermal reservoir An underground zone of porous rock containing hot water.

igneous rocks Rocks formed from the cooling and solidification of magma or lava.

intrusion An igneous rock body formed when molten igneous rock forces its way into surrounding host rocks and then cools; also the process of forming such an igneous rock body.

island arc A curving chain of volcanic islands formed at a compressional plate boundary.

Kimberlite pipe A vertical pipe-shaped intrusion of unusual igneous rocks that often contain diamonds.

lateral blast A hot, low-density mixture of rock debris, ash, and gases, generated by an explosion, that moves at high speed along the ground surface.

lava Magma or molten rock that has reached the surface; or its resulting solid rock after cooling.

lava dome A steep-sided, rounded extrusion of highly viscous lava, squeezed out from a volcanic vent.

lava lake A lake of molten lava in a volcanic crater or depression; refers to the solidified and partly solidified stages as well as to an active lava lake (Figure 61).

lava tube   A tunnel formed when the surface of a lava flow cools and solidifies and the still-molten interior lava flows through; also a hollow tube that remains when the interior lava drains away.

linear vent   A vent formed by a long fissure reaching the surface (in contrast to a single crater).

low-velocity layer   The zone in the upper mantle, about 60 to 250 kilometers in depth, in which seismic velocities are lower than in the overlying layers.

magma   Molten rock material with dissolved gases that forms igneous rocks on cooling; magma that reaches the surface is called lava.

magma chamber   An underground reservoir in the Earth's crust filled with magma, from which volcanic materials are derived.

magmatic fluids   Volcanic gases, especially water and carbon dioxide, dissolved in magma.

magnetic field   A region in which magnetic forces exist.

mantle   The zone of the Earth below the crust and above the core (to a depth of 3480 kilometers).

microearthquake   An earthquake that is not felt but is detectable by a seismograph.

mudflow   A flowing mixture of water-saturated mud and debris that moves downslope under the force of gravity.

neck   A vertical, pipelike intrusion that represents a former volcanic vent; usually used to describe an erosional remnant.

normal fault   An inclined fault in which the upper block moves relatively downward.

nuée ardente   A fast-moving, dense "glowing cloud" of hot volcanic ash and gas erupted from a volcano.

obsidian   A black or dark-colored volcanic glass, usually composed of rhyolite.

oceanic crust   The Earth's crust where it underlies the oceans, without the granite layer that forms continents.

olivine   An olive-green mineral composed of iron, magnesium, silicon, and oxygen.

ore   The naturally occurring material from which a mineral, or minerals, of commercial value can be extracted.

pahoehoe   A type of lava flow with a smooth, billowy, or undulating surface.

partial crystallization   The stage of cooling of magma when it is partly solid crystals and partly liquid rock.

partial melt   The stage of melting of rock when it is partly liquid rock and partly solid crystals.

pillow lava   Interconnected, sacklike bodies of lava formed under water.

plate tectonics   The theory that the Earth's crust is broken into about 12 large plates that slowly move about the surface.

plume   A rising column of magma from deep in the mantle responsible for hot-spot volcanoes; sometimes refers to ash or fume cloud.

pluton   A large igneous intrusion, formed at depth in the crust.

precipitate   A solid forming from a solution.

pumice   A form of volcanic glass so filled with gas bubble holes that it resembles a sponge and is very light.

pyroclastic flow   Mass of hot, dry rock fragments mixed with hot gases. Moves away from a volcano at high speeds. See also *nuée ardente.*

pyroclastics   Solid fragments formed by explosion or spraying from a volcanic vent; includes ash, cinders, and blocks.

quartz   An important rock-forming mineral composed of silicon and oxygen (SiO_2).

rhyolite   A fine-grained volcanic rock with the same composition as granite; although rhyolite and granite have the same composition, they differ in texture.

ridge, oceanic   A major submarine mountain range.

rift system   The oceanic ridges, over 60,000 kilometers in length, formed where plates are separating and new crust is being created; also their on-land equivalents like the East Africa Rift.

Ring of Fire   The regions of mountain-building earthquakes and volcanoes that surround the Pacific Ocean.

seafloor spreading   The mechanism by which new seafloor crust is created at oceanic ridges and slowly spreads away on the separating plates.

seamount   An isolated tall mountain on the seafloor, generally volcanic.

sedimentary mud   Loose fine-grained sediment with enough water to form soft mud.

seismic wave See *earthquake wave.*

seismograph An instrument that records the motions of the Earth's surface caused by seismic waves.

seismology The study of earthquakes, seismic waves, and the structure of the interior of the Earth.

shearing The motion of two surfaces sliding past one another.

shield volcano A gently sloping volcano in the shape of a flattened dome, built by flows of very fluid basaltic lava.

silica A chemical combination of silicon and oxygen.

silicate mineral A mineral largely composed of silicon and oxygen.

silicic Term used to describe silica-rich volcanic rock or magma.

stock A large igneous intrusion roughly circular in a horizontal plane.

stratovolcano A steep volcanic cone built both by lava flows and pyroclastic eruptions.

strike-slip fault A nearly vertical fault with side-slipping displacement.

subduction zone The zone of convergence of two tectonic plates, one of which usually overrides the other.

tephra A general term for all airfall pyroclastics from a volcano; sometimes used as a synonym for pyroclastics.

thermal gradient The rate of change of temperature with distance or depth.

thrust fault A gently inclined fault whose upper side moves relatively upward.

tidal wave See *tsunami.*

transform fault A strike-slip fault connecting the offsets of mid-ocean ridges.

tsunami A great sea wave produced by a submarine earthquake or volcanic eruption.

vein A mineral deposit precipitated in a rock fracture.

vent The opening at the Earth's surface through which volcanic materials issue forth.

viscosity A measure of resistance to flow in a liquid; water has a low viscosity while honey has a high viscosity.

volcanic front The line of volcanoes closest to the oceanic trench in island arcs like Japan.

wave-cut terrace A level surface formed by wave erosion of coastal rocks; may appear above sea level if uplifted.

APPENDIX A

The World's 101 Most Notorious Volcanoes

Activity, size, shape, beauty, danger, location, and the authors' preferences were used to select the following list. More complete catalogs of active volcanoes from which much of the data in this appendix are derived are listed in the Bibliography.

ANTARCTICA

Deception Island   A stratovolcano with a submarine caldera forming a horseshoe-shaped island. This snug harbor, protected from screaming antarctic storms, has recently been a base for various scientific expeditions. Small explosive eruptions interrupted expeditions' plans in 1967, 1969, and 1970.

Mount Erebus   A snow-and-ice-covered stratovolcano with an active lava lake in its summit crater. It was in eruption when first sighted in 1841 and has had several reported explosions since. The present lava lake, about 100 meters in diameter, apparently formed in the 1960s. Erebus is the world's farthest-south active volcano.

ATLANTIC OCEAN

Beerenberg   A stratovolcano with a caldera, on Jan Mayen Island north of Iceland. It is the farthest-north active volcano, and has erupted 5 times since 1633. The last eruption was in 1984.

La Palma   A complex volcano with a caldera and rift zones, on the west end of the Canary Islands. Lava flows have erupted 6 times since 1585; the last time was in 1971.

CARIBBEAN SEA

Mont Pelée   A stratovolcano with summit domes, on Martinique. The explosive eruption on May 8, 1902, generated a nuée ardente that swept down the mountainside and within minutes incinerated the town of Saint Pierre and its 28,000 inhabitants. Three other explosive eruptions have been recorded, the last in 1932. Photograph on page 83.

La Soufrière of Guadeloupe   A stratovolcano with a summit dome, on the southern part of Guadeloupe Island. It has erupted explosively about 10 times since 1400. The last eruption in 1976 prompted the evacuation of 70,000 people for several months, but turned out to be only minor explosions.

La Soufrière of St. Vincent   A stratovolcano with a crater lake. Its 7 eruptions since 1718 include 2 major explosive events. Evacuation in 1979 prevented a potential repeat of the tragedy of 1902, when 1600 deaths occurred, largely from nuées ardentes.

CHILE

Calbuco   A stratovolcano in southern Chile. Lava flows and explosive eruptions from the snow- and ice-filled crater caused major mudflows and the destruction of arable lands. It has erupted 9 times since 1837, the last time in 1961.

Llullaillaco   A stratovolcano in northern Chile. This is the world's highest active volcano with a summit elevation of 6723 meters. Of the 3 recorded eruptions during the 1800s, 2 were explosive and the other a lava flow from a side vent. Nevado Ojos del Salado (6886 meters), also in Chile, is higher, but has only steam vents and no recorded eruptions.

Villarrica   A stratovolcano in central Chile. About 20 explosive eruptions and 3 lava flows have occurred since 1558. The eruption in 1971 melted large volumes of snow and ice, and the resulting mudflows killed 15 people. The last eruption was in 1985.

COLOMBIA

Nevado del Ruiz   A high (5389 meter) stratovolcano in central Colombia. Mudflows from an earthquake or small eruption in 1845 killed about 1000 people. Another small-to-moderate eruption in 1985 melted part of the summit ice cap; the resulting mudflows caused about 25,000 fatalities (see pp. 241–243).

Puracé   A complex stratovolcano in southern Colombia. It has erupted explosively about 25 times since 1827, twice destroying arable land and causing deaths. The last eruption was in 1977.

COSTA RICA

Arenal   A stratovolcano in northwestern Costa Rica. Dormant until 1968, it burst into eruption with a strong explosion throwing huge blocks as far as 5 kilometers; the explosion was followed by nuées ardentes. This initial eruption killed 78 people. Activity has continued since with the extrusion of thick, slow-moving lava flows.

Irazú   A stratovolcano with a double crater, in central Costa Rica. It has erupted explosively about 15 times since 1723. The last major eruption lasted from 1963 until 1965; its numerous small to moderate ash falls were destructive to coffee plantations and a nuisance to the capital city of San Juan.

Poás   A stratovolcano with twin crater lakes, in central Costa Rica. It has erupted 20 times since 1834, generally with explosions of mud and water from the northern lake. The 1910 eruption shot a fountain of water more than 4 kilometers high. The last eruption was in 1988.

ECUADOR (ANDES MOUNTAINS)

Cotopaxi   A stratovolcano nearly 6000 meters high. It has had more than 50 eruptions since 1532 including major eruptions and lava flows. The 1877 eruption melted large volumes of snow and ice from the summit, causing mudflows that reached 100 kilometers down adjacent riverbeds. The last eruption was in 1942. Photograph on page 144.

Guagua Pichincha A stratovolcano with a caldera and a central cone. Although active from the 1500s to the 1800s, there has been only one small eruption in this century, in 1982. Forty centimeters of ash fell on the capital city of Quito in 1660; modern Quito climbs up the sides of this potentially dangerous volcano.

Reventador A stratovolcano east of the main ranges of the Andes. Although this mysterious volcano was not explored until 1931, it was apparently the source of some ash falls in Quito as far back as 1541. An important oil pipeline connecting the Amazon fields to the west coast of Ecuador now crosses its north slope. The last eruption was in 1976.

Sangay A 5230-meter-high snow- and ice-covered stratovolcano. Small explosive eruptions with occasional lava flows have kept this volcano in nearly continuous activity from 1728 to 1916, and from 1934 to 1988.

ECUADOR (GALAPAGOS ISLANDS)

Fernandina A shield volcano with a summit caldera. The most active of the Galapagos volcanoes, this uninhabited island was called Narborough in Darwin's chronicles. A major explosive eruption and 350-meter collapse of the caldera occurred in 1968. The last eruption was in 1988.

EL SALVADOR

Izalco A young stratovolcano born in 1770 on the south flank of Santa Ana Volcano in western El Salvador. It had nearly continuous small explosive eruptions until 1957 and was known as the Lighthouse of the Pacific. When a hotel was built nearby to view the frequent eruptions, the activity stopped. The last eruption was in 1966.

ETHIOPIA

Erta Alè A shield volcano with an active lava lake, in the rift valley of northern Ethiopia. Lava eruptions from fissures on the flank were observed in 1959–1960. The active lava lake discovered in 1967 has since been in constant eruption.

GREECE

Santorini   A stratovolcano with a submerged caldera, in the Aegean Sea. Its giant explosive eruption and caldera collapse in about 1500 B.C. buried Akroteri, an important Minoan city currently under excavation. The huge eruption and sudden sinking of the island's center beneath the sea may have been the source of the legend of Atlantis. The last eruption in 1950 formed a lava dome and thick lava flows on the islands within the caldera.

GUATEMALA

Atitlán   A stratovolcano on the south rim of a 20-kilometer-diameter caldera lake, in southwestern Guatemala. It has erupted with small to moderate explosions 11 times since 1469. The caldera lake, formed following immense prehistoric eruptions, is one of the most beautiful in the world.

Fuego   A stratovolcano in southwestern Guatemala whose name means fire. It has erupted more than 50 times since 1524, producing mostly explosions of ash but sometimes nuées ardentes and lava flows. The last eruption was in 1988.

Pacaya   A volcanic complex of two small stratovolcano cones and older lava domes, in southern Guatemala. It has erupted more than 30 times since 1565, generally with only explosions but with some lava flows in recent years. Eruptions have occurred nearly every year since 1965.

Santa Maria   A stratovolcano with a growing lava dome on its southwest slope, in western Guatemala. Its first eruption in historic time was in 1902; it produced a giant explosion of 5.5 cubic kilometers of pumice fragments and ash. A lava dome named Santiaguito began growing in the explosion crater in 1922 and has since been erupting intermittently. The last eruption was in 1988.

ICELAND

Askja   A complex volcano with a 10-kilometer-diameter caldera, in central Iceland. Although most of its 8 eruptions since the fourteenth century have been lava flows, the great eruption of 1875 exploded 2 cubic kilometers of ash over much of eastern Iceland. The resulting near-famine led many Icelanders to emigrate to the United States and Canada. The last eruption was in 1961.

Grímsvötn   A caldera in the Vatnajökull Icecap of south-central Iceland. It has erupted beneath the ice about 25 times since 1332, causing gigantic floods called glacial bursts. The sudden floods often exceed the flow volume of the Amazon River. The last eruption was in 1983.

Heimaey   A cinder cone with a thick blocky lava flow from its north side, in the Vestmann Islands off the south coast of Iceland. A 2-kilometer-long fissure opened near the fishing port of Heimaey in 1973. Cinders and ash soon covered much of the evacuated town of 5000 inhabitants, and the thick flow nearly closed off the harbor entrance. The courageous Icelanders returned to a better harbor, rebuilt their town, and even heat their hospital with steam from the cooling flows.

Hekla   A stratovolcano elongated by a northeast-trending rift system, in south-central Iceland. It has erupted 20 times since the settling of Iceland in A.D. 900, generally with ash explosions followed by lava flows. In medieval Europe, Hekla was considered the gate to Hell. The last eruption was in 1981.

Krafla   A complex volcano with a large central caldera, in northern Iceland. Dormant after a series of eruptions in 1724–1728, Krafla awakened in 1975 with small eruptions and episodes of extensive ground cracking. An eruption in 1977 also sprayed a small amount of lava out of a producing geothermal steam well, the only known case of an eruption from a man-made vent. Photographs on pages 47 and 48. The last eruption was in 1984.

Laki   A fissure zone more than 25 kilometers long, in south-central Iceland. Its single giant eruption in 1783 produced more than 12 cubic kilometers of lava, a historic record, filling two river valleys and covering more than 500 square kilometers. Stunted grass and fluorine poisoning from the accompanying volcanic gases starved and killed most of Iceland's livestock. The ensuing famine caused 10,000 deaths. Photograph on page 211; map on page 133.

Surtsey   A cinder-cone and lava-flow island on the south coast of Iceland. Born from the sea in 1963 and erupting until 1967, it has provided scientists a view of how land forms and plants and animals establish themselves in this new territory. Chapter 2 has photographs and additional information.

INDIAN OCEAN

Karthala A shield volcano with a summit caldera, on the southern part of Grand Comoro Island. It has erupted about 20 times since 1828, mainly lava flows that issue from the summit or rift zones. The last eruption was in 1977.

Piton de la Fournaise A shield volcano with a caldera, on the eastern part of Reunion Island. Sometimes called a sister to Hawaiian volcanoes because of the similarity of climate and volcanic nature, it has erupted lava flows more than 100 times since 1640. The last eruption was in 1988.

INDONESIA

Agung A stratovolcano in Bali considered in legend to be the navel of the world. Although it has erupted explosively only 4 times since 1808, the last eruption in 1963–1964 was of major proportions. High ash explosions affected world climate and nuées ardentes killed 2000 people.

Colo A low (508 meter) stratovolcano with a 2-kilometer-wide caldera and small crater lake on Una Una Island near Sulawesi (Celebes). A large explosive eruption occurred in 1983 just after the 7000 inhabitants of the island had been evacuated (see page 243).

Dieng A complex volcanic plateau with 26 cones and craters, in central Java. It has erupted about 10 times since 1825. The last eruption in 1979 consisted of poisonous gases that killed 150 people.

Galunggung A stratovolcano with a lava dome, in western Java. It has erupted only 4 times in history, but the first in 1822 produced a 22-kilometer-long mudflow that killed 4000 people. The last eruption, in 1982, killed 27 people.

Gamalama A stratovolcano island with multiple craters and crater lakes, west of Halmahera. It has erupted explosively more than 60 times since 1538, sometimes producing lava flows. The last eruption was in 1988.

Kelut A stratovolcano with a crater lake, in eastern Java. It has erupted 30 times since about A.D. 1000. The explosive eruptions eject the hot crater lake and cause widespread destruction. In the 1919 eruption, more than 100 villages were destroyed or damaged by mudflows that killed 5100 people. The last eruption was in 1967.

Krakatau   Stratovolcano islands around a submerged caldera, in the Sunda Strait between Sumatra and Java. The 1883 eruption was one of the largest natural explosions in recorded time. Sounds were heard for 4000 kilometers, the emitted ash and pumice blocks totaled 18 cubic kilometers, the 6-kilometer-diameter caldera collapsed, and the resulting tsunamis killed 36,000 people on the low shores of Java and Sumatra. The last eruption was in 1988. See pages 78, 212–214, and Figures 45–47.

Merapi   A stratovolcano with a summit lava dome in central Java whose name means mountain of fire. It has erupted more than 60 times since A.D. 1006, generally with explosions and nuées ardentes. The 1006 eruption caused so much death and destruction that the Hindu Rajah moved to Bali, and Mohammedanism took over Java. The last eruption was in 1986.

Papandajan   A complex stratovolcano in western Java. Although it has had only 2 historic eruptions, the explosions and landslides in 1772 destroyed 40 villages and killed 3000 people. The last eruption was in 1925.

Semeru   A stratovolcano with a summit lava dome, in eastern Java. Its nearly 70 eruptions, generally explosions that are sometimes accompanied by nuées ardentes and lava flows, make it one of Java's most active as well as its highest (3620 meters) volcano. The last eruption was in 1988.

Tambora   A stratovolcano with a summit caldera, on Sumbawa Island. Its giant eruption in 1815 exceeded the size and power of Krakatau. The explosion, followed by caldera collapse, is estimated to have produced about 40 cubic kilometers of ash and blocks. Ten thousand people were killed by the eruption and 80,000 starved in the resulting crop loss and famine. World climate may have been affected (see page 211).

ITALY

Etna   A transitional shield-to-stratovolcano in northeastern Sicily. It has erupted lava flows more than 150 times since activity was first recorded in 1500 B.C. Small to moderate explosive eruptions occur at the summit; one in 1979 took 9 lives. The last eruption was in 1987.

Stromboli   A stratovolcano island west of Italy. Known as the Lighthouse of the Mediterranean, it has been in almost continuous eruption for more than 2000 years. Small explosions of incandescent lava hurled up from the crater every 15 to 30 minutes are visible to ships passing by. Larger eruptions, some with lava flows, take place every several years.

Vesuvius   A complex stratovolcano east of Naples. Most famous for its A.D. 79 eruption that buried Pompeii, it has since erupted more than 50 times. Explosive eruptions are generally followed by lava flows. The last eruption was in 1944. Photograph on page 209.

Vulcano   A stratovolcano west of Italy. Legendary forge of Vulcan, this small island has provided the family name for all volcanoes. It has erupted explosively about 10 times since 200 B.C., the last time in 1888.

JAPAN

Asama   A complex stratovolcano in central Japan. It has erupted more than 100 times since A.D. 685, generally with a series of small explosions. In 1783 large nuées ardentes and mudflows buried villages, killing 1300 people. Scientists at the Asama Volcano Observatory, started in 1909, have found earthquake counts and locations to be useful in forecasting eruptions. The last eruption was in 1983.

Aso   A group of cinder cones and small stratovolcanoes within a 20-kilometer-diameter caldera. One vent has erupted more than 100 times since A.D. 796, generally as single, isolated explosions. Tourists visiting the rim of the active vent are sometimes killed by ejected blocks and bombs. The last eruption was in 1985.

Bandai   A stratovolcano with a caldera, in north-central Japan. It has erupted 6 times since A.D. 806, including the major explosions that formed the caldera in 1888. The debris from this explosive excavation, amounting to 1.2 cubic kilometers, swept down the north flank of Bandai, burying villages and killing 460 people.

Bayonnaise Rocks   Lava domes sometimes building ephemeral islands inside a submarine caldera southeast of Japan. This submarine volcanic center has erupted more than 10 times since it was first witnessed in 1896, sometimes building an island up to 95 meters high. A Japanese oceanographic ship investigating the area was destroyed by an explosion in 1952 with the loss of all 31 persons on board. The last eruption was in 1987.

Fuji   A classic stratovolcano in central Japan, the archetype of volcanic form. It has erupted ash and lava about 15 times since A.D. 781. The last eruption in 1707 was from a vent high on the southeast side that ejected 0.8 cubic kilometer of ash, blocks, and bombs. The finer ash reached Tokyo. Picture on page 78.

Oshima   A stratovolcano island with a caldera and a central cone, off the east coast of central Japan. It has erupted about 50 times since A.D. 684, sometimes explosively and sometimes with extensive lava flows. The last eruption was in 1988.

Sakura-zima   A stratovolcano forming a peninsula into Kagosima Bay, in southern Japan. One of the world's most active volcanoes, it has had thousands of small explosive eruptions since the first recorded one in A.D. 708. Many deaths occurred in 1476 and 1779, but sufficient warning from earthquakes kept the death toll to only a few persons in the giant eruption of 1914, which produced 0.6 cubic kilometer of ash and 1.6 cubic kilometers of thick lava flows. The last eruption was in 1988.

Tarumai   A complex stratovolcano with a lava dome, in northern Japan. It has erupted explosively about 35 times since 1667. A major eruption in 1909 discharged large volumes of ash and bombs, and was followed by the growth of the lava dome. The last eruption was in 1979.

Unzen   Multiple lava domes form this complex volcanic peninsula on the west coast of southern Japan. Although only 5 eruptions have been recorded since 860, the 1792 activity involved either an explosion or earthquake that triggered a 0.5-cubic-kilometer avalanche. The slide and resulting tsunami caused 14,000 deaths.

Usu   A stratovolcano with summit and flank lava domes, in northern Japan. Although it has erupted only 7 times since 1663, most of these eruptions have been explosive and destructive to life or land. In 1910, 1943–1944, and 1977–1979, large lava domes or ground surface uplifts, kilometers in diameter and tens to hundreds of meters high, were slowly forced upward.

MEXICO

Colima   A stratovolcano with a summit lava dome, in west-central Mexico. Its 16 eruptions since 1576 have been mostly explosive with some lava flows. The last eruption was in 1987.

El Chichón A small stratovolcano in Chiapas State in southern Mexico, dormant until 1982. Its sudden explosive eruption generated pyroclastic flows that killed about 2500 people and injected a huge cloud of dust and sulfuric acid aerosol into the stratosphere (see Chapter 14).

Parícutin A cinder cone in central Mexico. Born in a cornfield in 1943, it built a 410-meter-high cone with extensive lava fields during its brief life span. Most of the 1.3 cubic kilometers of ash and cinders, and much of the 0.7 cubic kilometer of lava, were produced in the first few years. The eruption ended in 1952.

Popocatépetl A snow-capped stratovolcano dominating the skyline south of Mexico City. It erupted with small explosions 11 times between 1512 and 1697. Since a major explosion in 1720 only 3 small eruptions have occurred, the last in 1943.

NEW ZEALAND

Ngauruhoe A stratovolcano with a near perfect cone, in central North Island. It has had more than 50 explosive eruptions since 1839, some with small nuées ardentes. The latest eruption was in 1975. Photograph on page 154.

Ruapehu A stratovolcano with a hot crater lake, in central North Island. There have been more than 30 small explosions of steam and ash from the crater lake since 1861. Mudflows from the erupting lake occasionally flood adjacent valleys. One such flow on Christmas Eve in 1953 swept away a railroad bridge, wrecking the Wellington-Auckland Express and causing 151 deaths. The latest eruption was in 1988. Photograph on page 154.

Tarawera A volcanic complex of rhyolite domes, in central North Island. A great eruption along a 17-kilometer-long fissure in 1886 ejected 1.3 cubic kilometers of basaltic ash and hot mud, burying three villages and killing more than 150 persons. From 1900 to 1904 Waimangu (black water) Geyser erupted in one of the craters formed along the 1886 fissure. Occasional geyser bursts of 400 to 500 meters during that time were the highest ever recorded.

White Island A stratovolcano in the Bay of Plenty north of New Zealand, with a large horseshoe-shaped crater. About 35 small to moderate explosive eruptions have occurred since 1826. Eleven men were killed and a sulfur works destroyed in the 1914 eruption and landslide. The last eruption was in 1988.

NICARAGUA

Cerro Negro A cinder cone in western Nicaragua whose name means black hill. Born in 1850, it has erupted about 15 times in its brief life span. Explosive eruptions from the central crater are often accompanied by lava flows that issue from near the base of the cinder cone. The last eruption was in 1971. Photograph on page 71.

Cosegüina A stratovolcano with a central caldera lake, in western Nicaragua. A single major explosive eruption occurred in 1835 that scattered ash throughout Central America and southern Mexico. The ash cloud blotted out the sun over an area 300 kilometers wide.

Masaya A caldera with small central stratovolcanoes in southwestern Nicaragua. It has erupted 20 times since 1524 with varied activity including explosions, lava flows, and lava lakes. The last eruption was in 1987. Photograph on page 148.

PACIFIC OCEAN

Ambrym A stratovolcano within a huge caldera in the New Hebrides Islands. Although the record is incomplete, it has been very active with many ash explosions and lava flows since its discovery in 1774. The last eruption was in 1988.

Falcon A submarine volcano in the Tonga Islands, famous for its appearing and disappearing islands. Cinder-cone islands formed during eruptions in 1885 and 1927 have been washed away by the sea into shallow banks. An island formed from 1927 to 1933 grew to 3 kilometers in diameter and 150 meters in height. The last eruption was in 1970.

Macdonald Seamount A submarine volcano at the southeast end of the Austral Islands and Seamounts in the South Pacific. Its summit is about 30 meters below sea level. This volcano was discovered to be active in 1967, when noises from it were picked up by distant hydrophones. In 1987 an oceanographic expedition sailing over the seamount witnessed the eruption of large gas bubbles and small fragments of basalt. Seismometers and hydrophones indicate that the eruptions have continued into 1988.

Pagan A stratovolcano in the Mariana Islands of the western Pacific Ocean. After 4 small eruptions between 1909 and 1925, a large explosive eruption in 1981 lofted an ash cloud to 20 kilometers above the island. Smaller eruptions have occurred since, the last in 1988.

Raoul   A complex stratovolcano island with a caldera and crater lakes, in the Kermadec Islands north of New Zealand. This remote volcano is noteworthy because a research seismic station there, part of a worldwide net, gave warning of the 1964 eruption by recording a forerunning swarm of local earthquakes.

Yasour   A stratovolcano in the New Hebrides Islands. It has been in almost constant mild eruption since its discovery in 1774. Numerous small explosions hurl lava bombs 20 to 200 meters in the air.

PAPUA NEW GUINEA

Karkar   A stratovolcano island with a summit caldera, off the north coast of Papua New Guinea. It has erupted about 10 times since 1643. The eruption in 1979 took the lives of volcanologists Robin Cooke and Elias Ravian. The last eruption was in 1981.

Lamington   A stratovolcano with a lava dome, in eastern Papua New Guinea. This dormant volcano suddenly exploded in 1951. The pyroclastic flows devastated more than 200 square kilometers and killed about 3000 people. A 500-meter-high lava dome grew in the explosion crater from 1951 to 1956. The volcano has been quiet since then.

Manam   A 1300-meter-high stratovolcano that forms a circular island 10 kilometers in diameter, off the north coast of Papua New Guinea. Intermittent small explosive eruptions have occurred frequently from 1974 to 1988.

Rabaul   A group of small volcanoes around the rim of a caldera bay on New Britain Island. Although the vents around Rabaul Harbour have erupted only 6 times since 1767, the violent explosive eruption in 1937 formed Vulcan crater, generated tsunamis, and killed 500 people. The last eruption was in 1943. See page 241 and Figure 137.

PERU

El Misti   A classic stratovolcano rising high above the city of Arequipa. Small explosive eruptions, the last in 1870, and gentle steaming characterize its historic activity. It is noted for its beauty rather than its habits.

PHILIPPINES

Mayon   A classic stratovolcano cone in the central Philippines. It has erupted explosively more than 40 times since 1616, often producing nuées ardentes and lava flows. The region is densely populated and at least 8 eruptions have caused fatalities. The last eruption was in 1984. Photograph on page 146.

Taal   A stratovolcano island within a huge caldera lake, in the central Philippines. It has erupted more than 30 times since 1572, generally explosions that are sometimes accompanied by tsunamis in the lake. This killer volcano took many lives in 1716, 1749, 1754, 1874, 1911, and 1965. The last eruption was in 1977.

TANZANIA

Ol Doinyo Lengai   A stratovolcano in northern Tanzania whose name means Mountain of God. Although it has erupted more than 10 times since 1880, this volcano is more famous to science for its unusual lava flows composed in part of sodium carbonate. The last eruption was in 1988. Photograph on page 207.

UNION OF SOVIET SOCIALIST REPUBLICS (KAMCHATKA)

Bezymianny   A complex stratovolcano in central Kamchatka. Small explosive eruptions beginning in 1955 climaxed in a gigantic explosion in 1956, forming a mushroom cloud 35 kilometers high (photograph on page 84). The thick, hot ash-flow deposits formed the Valley of Ten Thousand Smokes of Kamchatka, a feature similar to that created by the Katmai eruption in Alaska in 1912. The last eruption was in 1988.

Karymsky   A stratovolcano within an ancient caldera, in southeast Kamchatka. Its 35 eruptions since 1771 have been mostly explosive. The last eruption was in 1982.

Kliuchevskoi   A classic stratovolcano in central Kamchatka. It has erupted explosively more than 75 times since 1697, often producing lava flows. The last eruption was in 1988.

Tolbachik   A stratovolcano with a caldera, in central Kamchatka. After about 20 moderate eruptions since 1740, it produced a giant fissure eruption in 1975 that built several large cinder cones and major lava flows totaling nearly 2 cubic kilometers in volume. Forerunning earthquake swarms led to a prediction of the time and place of the 1975 eruption, precise enough that TV camera crews were on location for the outbreak. Photograph on page 240.

UNITED STATES (ALASKA)

Augustine A stratovolcano island with a summit lava dome, in the Cook Inlet, southern Alaska. It has erupted explosively 7 times since 1812. Dangers from major ash falls or volcanically generated tsunamis worry the offshore oil developers located nearby. The last eruption was in 1986.

Katmai A complex stratovolcano with a summit caldera and lake, on the Alaska Peninsula. The 1912 eruption of Katmai was among the world's largest in historic time. In 2 days thick ash deposits covered a huge area, and a glowing avalanche filled a valley 3 kilometers wide and 20 kilometers long creating the Valley of Ten Thousand Smokes. The summit caldera, 5 kilometers in diameter, formed by collapse during the eruption. The total volume of the ash and glowing avalanche was 30 cubic kilometers. Although most of the valley "smokes" (steam vents) are now dead, Mount Trident, a new vent on the west flank of Katmai, became active in 1949 and has exploded and extruded thick lava flows several times. The last eruption of Trident was in 1974.

Pavlof A stratovolcano on the Alaska Peninsula (Figure 79). It has had more than 40 periods of small to moderate explosive eruptions since 1790. The latest one began in 1986 and was continuing in 1988.

Shishaldin A classic stratovolcano cone in the eastern Aleutian Islands. It has a record of about 30 small to moderate explosive eruptions since 1775. Its sharp, snow-covered peak often has a plume of volcanic gases. The last eruption was in 1987.

UNITED STATES (CASCADE RANGE)

Lassen Peak A stratovolcano with a summit lava dome, in northern California. It had a series of explosive eruptions in 1914–1915 that culminated in hot avalanches in May 1915. Small explosions occurred again in 1917. Photograph on page 147.

Mount Rainier A massive, glacier-covered stratovolcano near Seattle, Washington. It has been dormant since about 1850, when a small explosive eruption apparently occurred. Small steam vents issue from the edges of the snow-and-ice-filled summit crater. Photograph on page 155.

Mount St. Helens A snow-covered stratovolcano in southern Washington known for its beauty and serenity before its gigantic explosive eruption on May 18, 1980. A directed blast leveled 500 square kilometers of forest, and a major debris avalanche filled a valley for 25 kilometers. The 2950-meter-high summit was lowered by 400 meters, forming a deep horseshoe crater facing north. About 57 people were killed, including David Johnston, a volcanologist. The last eruption was in 1986. Chapter 4 has photographs and additional information.

UNITED STATES (HAWAII)

Kilauea A shield volcano with a summit caldera, on the Island of Hawaii. Famous for its active lava lake during the 1800s and early 1900s, it has also erupted extensive lava flows more than 50 times from both the summit and rift zones. The last eruption was in 1989. Chapter 6 has photographs and additional information on Kilauea's Puu Oo eruption, which began in 1983.

Mauna Loa A massive shield volcano with a summit caldera, on the Island of Hawaii. It has erupted large lava flows from both the summit and rift zones 38 times since 1832, producing a total of nearly 4 cubic kilometers of basalt. The last eruption was in 1984. Photograph on page 153; map on page 238.

ZAIRE

Nyamuragira A shield volcano with a summit caldera, in eastern Zaire. It has erupted more than 20 times since 1894, including lava lake activity from 1921 to 1938. The last eruption was in 1988.

Nyiragongo A stratovolcano with a summit caldera, in eastern Zaire. It has erupted about 15 times since 1884, including lava lake activity from 1935 to 1977. A major fissure eruption on the south flank in 1977 drained the lava lake and rapidly covered an area of several square kilometers with very fluid lavas. About 300 people were killed by these flows. The last eruption was in 1982. See Color Plate 24.

APPENDIX B

Volcano Information Centers of the World

Volcanoes change, and so do the people and institutions who study them. The information centers listed in this appendix are those whose staffs have a major interest in active volcanism. The list is probably not complete, but it does provide contacts for obtaining data on active volcanoes in most areas of the world. The Scientific Event Alert Network (see United States listing) publishes a monthly Bulletin summarizing current volcanic events. It is the best single data source on worldwide volcanic activity.

AUSTRALIA

Bureau of Mineral Resources
Canberra, ACT, 2601
Australia

AZORES

Department of Geology
Azores University
Horta, Azores

CAMEROON

Dept. des Sciences de la Terre
Université de Yaoundé
B.P. 812
Yaoundé, Cameroon

CANADA

Geological Survey of Canada
100 W. Pender St.
Vancouver, BC, Canada

CHILE

Departamento de Geología y
  Geofísica
Universidad de Chile
Casilla 13518 Correo 21
Santiago, Chile

Universidad del Norte
Casilla 1280
Antofagasta, Chile

COLOMBIA

Observatorio Vulcanológico Nacional
Apartado Aereo 1296
Manizales, Colombia

COSTA RICA

Escuela Centroamericana de Geología
Universidad de Costa Rica
Apartado 35 UCR
San José, Costa Rica

Instituto Costarricense de
  Electricidad
Apartado 10032
San José, Costa Rica

Observatorio Vulcanológico y
  Sismológico de Costa Rica
Escuela de Ciencias Geográficas
Universidad Nacional
Heredia, Costa Rica

ECUADOR

Charles Darwin Research Station
Galapagos Islands
Casilla 58-39
Guayaquil, Ecuador

Departamento de Geología
Escuela Politécnica Nacional
Casilla 2759
Quito, Ecuador

EL SALVADOR

Centro de Investigaciones
  Geotécnicas
Apartado 06-109
San Salvador, El Salvador

ENGLAND

British Museum
Cromwell Road
London SW7 5BD, England

Department of Mineralogy and
  Petrology
University of Cambridge
Downing Place
Cambridge CB2 3EW, England

Institute of Geological Sciences
154 Clerkenwell Road
London EC1R 5DU, England

University of London Observatory
Mill Hill Park
London NW7 2QS, England

ETHIOPIA

Geophysical Observatory
University of Addis Ababa
P.O. Box 1176
Addis Ababa, Ethiopia

FRANCE

Centre de Recherches
  Volcanologiques
5 Rue Kessler
63038 Clermont-Ferrand, France

Equipé Vulcain
B.P. 5
68700 Cernay, France

Laboratoire de Volcanologie
C.F.R. (C.N.R.S.)
91190 Gif-sur-Yvette, France

Observatoires Volcanologiques
Institut de Physique du Globe de Paris
Tour 14, 4, place Jussieu
75252 Paris Cedex 05, France

GERMANY

Institut für Mineralogie
Ruhr-Universität
Postfach 102148
D-4630 Bochum 1, Germany

Mineralogisches Institut
Albert-Ludwigs Universität
D-7800 Freiburg, Germany

Mineralogisch-Petrographisches
  Institut
Universität Tübingen
Wilhelmstrasse 56
D-74 Tübingen, Germany

GUATEMALA

INSIVUMEH
7A Avenida 14-57, Zona 13
Ciudad de Guatemala, Guatemala

Instituto Geográfico Nacional
Avenida las Américas 5-76, Zona 13
Ciudad de Guatemala, Guatemala

ICELAND

Nordic Volcanological Institute
University of Iceland
101 Reykjavík, Iceland

INDONESIA

Volcanological Survey of Indonesia
Diponegoro 57
Bandung, Indonesia

ITALY

Centro di Studio per la Geologia
  Tecnica
Via Eudossiana 18
Roma, Italy

Dipartimento di Geofisica e
  Vulcanologia
Largo S. Marcellino 10
80138 Napoli, Italy

Istituto di Vulcanologia
Corso Italia 55
95129 Catania, Italy

Instituto Internazionale di
  Vulcanologia
Viale Regina Margherita 6
95123 Catania, Italy

Osservatorio Vesuviano
Via Manzoni 239
80100 Napoli, Italy

JAPAN

Departments of Geology and
  Geophysics
Hokkaido University
Kita-ku
Sapporo 060, Japan

Department of Geophysics
Kyoto University
Uji, Kyoto 611, Japan

Earthquake Research Institute
University of Tokyo
Bunkyo-ku
Tokyo 113, Japan

Office of Volcanic Observation
Seismological Division
Japan Meteorological Agency
1-3-4 Otemachi, Chiyoda-ku
Tokyo 100, Japan

MÉXICO

Instituto de Geofísica
Universidad Nacional Autónoma de
    México
México 20, D.F., México

NEW ZEALAND

Geology Department
University of Canterbury
Christchurch 1, New Zealand

Geology Department
Victoria University
Private Bag
Wellington, New Zealand

New Zealand Geological Survey
P.O. Box 499
Rotorua, New Zealand

NICARAGUA

Instituto de Investigaciones Sísmicas
Apartado 1761
Managua, Nicaragua

PAPUA NEW GUINEA

Rabaul Volcano Observatory
Geological Survey of Papua New
    Guinea
P.O. Box 386
Rabaul, Papua New Guinea

PERU

Departamento de Geología
Universidad Nacional de San Agustín
Casilla 1203
Arequipa, Peru

PHILIPPINES

Philippine Institute of Volcanology
    and Seismology
6th Floor, Hizon Building
29 Quezon Avenue
Quezon City, Philippines

RÉUNION ISLAND

Laboratoire de Géologie
Centre Universitaire de la Réunion
Réunion Island

Observatoire Volcanologique du
    Piton de la Fournaise
14 R.N.3, 27ème km
97418 La Plaine des Cafres
Réunion Island

SOLOMON ISLANDS

Geological Survey
G.P.O. Box G 24
Honiara, Solomon Islands

SPAIN

Departamento de Petrología y
    Geoquímica
Ciudad Universitaria
Madrid 3, Spain

TAHITI

Laboratoire de Géophysique
B.P. 640
Papeete, Tahiti

UNION OF SOVIET SOCIALIST REPUBLICS

Institute of Volcanology
Piip Avenue 9, Petropavlovsk
Kamchatsky 683006, USSR

World Data Center B1
Molodezhnaya 3
Moscow 117 296, USSR

UNITED STATES

Geophysical Institute
University of Alaska
Fairbanks, Alaska 99701, USA

Office of Earthquakes, Volcanoes
and Engineering
U.S. Geological Survey
Reston, Virginia 22092, USA

Scientific Event Alert Network
Smithsonian Institution
Washington, D.C. 20560, USA

U.S. Geological Survey
Cascades Volcano Observatory
5400 MacArthur Blvd.
Vancouver, Washington 98661, USA

U.S. Geological Survey
Hawaiian Volcano Observatory
P.O. Box 51, Hawaii National Park
Hawaii 96718, USA

World Data Center A for Solid-Earth
Geophysics, Environmental Data
and Information Service, NOAA
Boulder, Colorado 80303, USA

VANUATU

Geological Survey Department
Port Vila, Vanuatu

WEST INDIES

Observatoire Volcanologique de la
Mont Pelée
Fond, 11 Denis
97250 St. Pierre, Martinique, West
Indies

Observatoire Volcanologique de la
Soufrière
97120 St Claude
Guadeloupe, West Indies

Seismic Research Unit
University of the West Indies
St. Augustine
Trinidad, West Indies

ZAIRE

Department of Seismology
I.R.S.
Lwiro, D/S Bukavu (Kivu)
Zaire

APPENDIX C

. . . .

Metric – English Conversion Table

Length

1 centimeter	0.3937 inch
1 inch	2.5400 centimeters
1 meter	3.2808 feet
1 foot	0.3048 meter
1 meter	1.0936 yards
1 yard	0.9144 meter
1 kilometer	0.6214 mile
1 kilometer	3281 feet
1 mile	1.6093 kilometers

Area

1 square centimeter	0.1550 square inch
1 square inch	6.452 square centimeters
1 square meter	10.764 square feet
1 square meter	1.1960 square yards
1 square foot	0.0929 square meter
1 square kilometer	0.3861 square mile
1 square mile	2.590 square kilometers

Volume

1 cubic centimeter	0.0610 cubic inch
1 cubic inch	16.3872 cubic centimeters
1 cubic meter	35.314 cubic feet
1 cubic foot	0.02832 cubic meter
1 cubic meter	1.3079 cubic yards
1 cubic yard	0.7646 cubic meter

Mass	
1 gram	0.03527 ounce
1 ounce	28.3495 grams
1 kilogram	2.20462 pounds
1 pound	0.45359 kilogram
Density	
1 gram/cubic centimeter	62.4280 pounds/cubic foot
Pressure	
1 kilogram/square centimeter	0.96784 atmosphere
1 kilogram/square centimeter	0.98067 bar
1 kilogram/square centimeter	14.2233 pounds/square inch
1 bar	0.98692 atmosphere
1 atmosphere	1.0332 kilogram/square cm
Temperature	
(Celsius $\times$ 9/5) + 32	Fahrenheit
(Fahrenheit $-$ 32) $\times$ 5/9	Celsius
Energy	
1 erg	2.39006×10^{-8} gram calorie
1 joule	10^{7} ergs
Explosion equivalent to 1000 tons of TNT	4×10^{19} ergs
Power	
1 watt	10^{7} ergs/second
1 watt	0.001341 horsepower

Bibliography

· · · · · · · · · · · · ·

Chapter 1. Seams of the Earth

Cox, Allen, ed. *Plate Tectonics and Geomagnetic Reversals.* New York: W. H. Freeman and Company, 1973.

Press, Frank, and Raymond Siever. *Earth.* New York: W. H. Freeman and Company, Fourth Edition, 1986.

Uyeda, Seiya. *The New View of the Earth.* New York: W. H. Freeman and Company, 1978.

Wilson, Tuzo, ed. *Continents Adrift and Continents Aground.* Readings from Scientific American. New York: W. H. Freeman and Company, 1963–1976.

Wyllie, Peter J. *The Way the Earth Works.* New York: John Wiley and Sons, 1976.

Chapter 2. Surtsey, Iceland

Thorarinsson, Sigurdur. "Surtsey: Island Born of Fire." *National Geographic Magazine*, May 1965, pp. 713–26.

Thorarinsson, Sigurdur. *Surtsey.* New York: Viking Press, 1967.

Chapter 3. Fire Under the Sea

Francheteau, Jean. "The Oceanic Crust." *Scientific American*, September 1983.

Heezen, Bruce, and Charles Hollister. *The Face of the Deep.* New York: Oxford University Press, 1971.

Heezen, Bruce, Marie Tharp, and M. Ewing. *The Floors of the*

Oceans: I. The North Atlantic. Geological Society of America, Special Paper 65, 1959.

Macdonald, Ken C., and Bruce P. Luyendyk. "The Crest of the East Pacific Rise." *Scientific American,* May 1981.

Menard, H.W. *Islands.* New York: Scientific American Library, W. H. Freeman and Co., 1986.

Menard, H. W. *Marine Geology of the Pacific.* New York: McGraw-Hill, 1964.

Chapter 4. Mount St. Helens

Decker, Robert, and Barbara Decker. "The Eruptions of Mount St. Helens." *Scientific American,* March 1981.

Lipman, Peter W., and Donal R. Mullineaux, eds. *The 1980 Eruptions of Mount St. Helens.* U.S. Geological Survey, Professional Paper 1250, 1981.

Chapter 5. Ring of Fire

Dewey, John F., and John M. Bird. "Mountain Belts and the New Global Tectonics." *Journal of Geophysical Research* 75, No. 14, 1970, pp. 2625–47.

Harris, Stephen. *Fire Mountains of the West.* Missoula, Mont.: Mountain Press, 1987.

Sugimura, A., and Seiya Uyeda. *Island Arcs: Japan and Its Environs.* Amsterdam: Elsevier, 1973.

Toksoz, M. Nafi. "The Subduction of the Lithosphere." *Scientific American,* November 1975, pp. 88–98.

Chapter 6. Kilauea, Hawaii

Decker, Robert, Thomas Wright, and Peter Stauffer, eds. *Volcanism in Hawaii.* U.S. Geological Survey, Professional Paper 1350, 2 vols., 1987.

Heliker, Christina, et al. "Volcano Monitoring at the U.S. Geological Survey's Hawaiian Volcano Observatory." *Earthquakes and Volcanoes* 18, No. 1, 1986, pp. 1–72.

Macdonald, Gordon A., Agatin T. Abbott, and Frank L. Peterson. *Volcanoes in the Sea.* Honolulu: University of Hawaii Press, 1983.

Macdonald, Gordon A., and Douglass Hubbard. *Volcanoes of the National Parks of Hawaii.* Hawaii: Hawaii Natural History Association, 1982.

Stearns, Harold T. *Geology of the State of Hawaii.* Palo Alto, Calif.: Pacific Books, Second Edition, 1985.

Chapter 7. Hot Spots

Burke, Kevin, and J. Tuzo Wilson. "Hot Spots on the Earth's Surface." *Scientific American,* August 1976, pp. 46–57.

Clague, David, and C. Brent Dalrymple. "The Hawaiian-Emperor Volcanic Chain." *Volcanism in Hawaii.* U.S. Geological Survey, Professional Paper 1350, pp. 5–54.

Dalrymple, G. Brent, E. A. Silver, and E. D. Jackson. "Origin of the Hawaiian Islands." *American Scientist* 61, No. 3, 1973, pp. 294–308.

Morgan, W. J. "Deep Mantle Convection Plumes and Plate Motions." *American Association of Petroleum Geologists Bulletin* 56, No. 1, 1972, pp. 203–13.

Chapter 8. Lava, Ash, and Bombs

Cas, R.A.F., and J. V. Wright. *Volcanic Successions.* London: Allen & Unwin, 1987.

Fisher, R. V., and H.-U. Schmincke. *Pyroclastic Rocks.* Berlin: Springer-Verlag, 1984.

Francis, Peter. *Volcanoes.* Middlesex, England: Penguin Books, 1976.

Macdonald, Gordon A. *Volcanoes.* Englewood Cliffs, N.J.: Prentice-Hall, 1972.

Williams, Howel, and A. R. McBirney. *Volcanology.* San Francisco: Freeman, Cooper and Co., 1979.

Chapter 9. Cones and Craters

Bullard, Fred M. *Volcanoes of the Earth.* Austin: University of Texas Press, 1984.

Editors of Time-Life Books. *Volcano.* Chicago, Ill.: Time-Life Books, 1982.

Green, Jack, and Nicholas M. Short, eds. *Volcanic Landforms and Surface Features.* New York: Springer-Verlag, 1971.

Krafft, Maurice, and Katia Krafft. *Volcanoes: Earth's Awakening.* Maplewood, N.J.: Hammond, 1980.

Chapter 10. Roots of Volcanoes

Decker, Robert, and Barbara Decker, eds. *Volcanoes and the Earth's Interior.* Readings from Scientific American. New York: W. H. Freeman and Company, 1975–1982.

Elder, John. *The Bowels of the Earth*. Oxford: Oxford University Press, 1978.

Wyllie, Peter. "The Earth's Mantle." *Scientific American*, March 1975, pp. 50–57.

Chapter 11. Origin of the Sea and Air

Anderson, A. T. "Some Basaltic and Andesitic Gases." *Reviews of Geophysics and Space Physics* 13, 1975, pp. 37–55.

Holland, H. D. *The Chemical Evolution of the Atmosphere and Oceans*. Princeton, N.J.: Princeton University Press, 1984.

Stoiber, R. E., and A. Jepsen. "Sulfur Dioxide Contributions to the Atmosphere by Volcanoes." *Science* 182, 1973, pp. 577–78.

Chapter 12. Volcanic Power

Barnea, Joseph. "Geothermal Power." *Scientific American*, January 1972, pp. 70–77.

Kruger, P., and C. Otte, eds. *Geothermal Energy*. Stanford, Calif.: Stanford University Press, 1973.

Muffler, L. J. P., ed. *Assessment of Geothermal Resources of the United States — 1978*. U.S. Geological Survey Circular 790, 1979.

Rybach, L., and L. J. P. Muffler, *Geothermal Systems: Principles and Case Histories*. New York: John Wiley and Sons, 1981.

Chapter 13. Volcanic Treasures

Boyd, F. R., and Henry O. A. Meyer, eds. *Kimberlites, Diatremes, and Diamonds: Their Geology, Petrology, and Geochemistry*. Washington, D.C.: American Geophysical Union, 1979.

Koski, Randolph A., et al. "Hydrothermal Processes and Massive Sulfide Deposits on the Juan de Fuca Ridge and Other Northeast Pacific Spreading Axes." *Circum Pacific Council for Energy and Mineral Resources Earth Science Series* 6, 1987, pp. 621–38.

Park, Charles F., Jr., and Roy A. MacDiarmid. *Ore Deposits*. New York: W. H. Freeman and Company, 1975.

Rona, Peter A. "Plate Tectonics and Mineral Resources." *Scientific American*, July 1973, pp. 86–95.

Chapter 14. Volcanoes and Climate

Lamb, H. H. *Climate: Present, Past, and Future*. London: Methuen, 1972.

Pollack, James B., Owen B. Toon, Carl Sagan, Audrey Summers,

Betty Baldwin, and Warren Van Camp. "Volcanic Explosions and Climatic Change: A Theoretical Assessment." *Journal of Geophysical Research* 81, No. 6, 1976, pp. 1071–83.

Rampino, Michael, et al. "Volcanic Winters." *Annual Review of Earth and Planetary Sciences*, 16, 1988, pp. 73–99.

Stommel, Henry, and Elizabeth Stommel. "The Year Without a \ Summer." *Scientific American*, June 1979, pp. 176–80.

Chapter 15. Forecasting Volcanic Eruptions

Blong, R. J. *Volcanic Hazards.* Orlando, Fla.: Academic Press, 1984.

Crandell, Dwight R., and Donal R. Mullineaux, *Potential Hazards from Future Eruptions of Mount St. Helens Volcano, Washington.* U.S. Geological Survey Bulletin 1383-C. U.S. Government Printing Office, Washington, D.C., 1978.

Decker, R. W. "Forecasting Volcanic Eruptions." *Annual Review Earth and Planetary Sciences* 14, 1986, pp. 267–91.

Geophysics Study Committee, Geophysics Research Board, National Research Council. *Geophysical Predictions.* Washington, D.C.: National Academy of Sciences, 1978.

Minakami, T., ed. *Surveillance and Prediction of Volcanic Activity.* Paris: UNESCO, Earth Science Monographs, 1972.

Appendix A. The World's 101 Most Notorious Volcanoes

International Association of Volcanology and Chemistry of the Earth's Interior. *Catalog of Active Volcanoes of the World, Parts I–XXII.* Rome, Italy, 1951–1975.

Simkin, Tom, et al. *Volcanoes of the World.* Washington, D.C.: Smithsonian Institution, 1981.

Smithsonian Institution. *Scientific Event Alert Network Bulletin* 1–14. Washington, D.C., 1976–1989.

Volcanological Society of Japan. *Bulletin of Volcanic Eruptions* 1–25. Tokyo, Japan, 1963–1988.

Index